Know Your Money

Helping Young Adults Make Smart
Money Decisions for Daily Living

Joel Read

 iUniverse®

KNOW YOUR MONEY
HELPING YOUNG ADULTS MAKE SMART MONEY
DECISIONS FOR DAILY LIVING

iUniverse books may be ordered through booksellers or by contacting:

iUniverse
1663 Liberty Drive
Bloomington, IN 47403
www.iuniverse.com
1-800-Authors (1-800-288-4677)

ISBN: 978-1-4917-4734-6 (sc)
ISBN: 978-1-4917-4735-3 (hc)
ISBN: 978-1-4917-4736-0 (e)

Library of Congress Control Number: 2014917017

Printed in the United States of America.

iUniverse rev. date: 10/21/2014

Contents

To my lovely wife, Lori, and our four children: Ashley, Kyle, Eric, and Casey.

Over the years, many family hours have been spent talking about life's challenges and how to handle them. As parents, we've helped our children develop their own unique approaches to handling their money and encouraged them to prepare to move out on their own. Now they've flown the coop, and the house is a lot quieter! Best wishes to all our children—and today's generation of young adults—as they prepare for their financial independence.

To my friends: Doug Frank, Hank Belusa, John Farmakis, Don Beck and Scott Bechler.

A special thank-you to my friends: I appreciated your constant encouragement throughout the creative process of developing materials and writing this book.

Preface

It's only money. No need to be afraid of it. Do you know how to take control of it? If you do, you can save your worrying for something else.

As a young adult, you've spent twelve or more years gaining an education for a career but very little time learning about how to manage the money that career will provide. With just a few tips, you can avoid many common mistakes, easily gain control of your money, and become more independent. Young adults need to take some major action for themselves, including pursuing a career doing what they love and learning to manage their money. I hope this book helps today's young adults to

- confidently discuss money issues with others;
- make good financial choices;
- become more independent without being slaves to debt;
- be prepared for tough economic times (they will come at some point); and
- worry less about money and spend more time enjoying life's journey.

You already have the skills you need to take control of your money and become a financially independent adult. The key is to *know your money*. No matter what stage of life you're in, you can avoid common mistakes and plan where you want to go in life. Your financial success grows when you adopt good money habits and live within your means—no debts, no frets.

Best wishes for a successful transition to financial independence.

Joel Read
Author and Parent

Prologue

Preparing for the Journey

As a young adult, you have two major life-changing transitions before you: selecting a career and moving out of your parents' house. Being independent is a dream, and this is an exciting time—but also an anxious time, given how uncertain things will be for the next few years. Chances are, you've already heard all the traditional advice:

- "Figure out what you love to do, and make a career out of it. If you love what you do, it isn't work."
- "Money doesn't buy happiness. More money may let you buy more stuff, but when will you stop wanting even more stuff? Be content in life with what you have."
- "As an adult, you are responsible for your actions. That includes money, so aspire to live within your means."

To succeed at these, you must learn who you are as a person. Not all careers will make you happy, and each offers different earning potential—that is, money. Your priority should be on selecting a career you are passionate about and avoiding the pursuit of different careers just for the sake of bigger bucks. To enable this, you must know how to handle the money you do have, whether a lot or a little.

Many young adults want to live independently, but they don't understand the key financial fundamentals for daily living. This book will help you figure out the answers to important questions, so you can make smart money decisions for daily living:

- Are you a saver or a spender?
- What info do you need for your federal tax filing?
- What should you look for before you sign an apartment lease?
- What's the difference between debit and credit cards?
- How is your credit score calculated?
- What's the real cost of buying something when you use a loan to buy it?
- Does your auto insurance cover your friend if you loan him or her your car?
- How much should you save for a rainy day before saving for retirement?
- When do you need a new budget?
- How do you balance your checkbook?

In each chapter, solve the exercises, spend time thinking about the discussion topics and conclusions, and look for the "know your money" tips on avoiding common pitfalls. At the end of the book is a recap of the key points from each chapter to help you remember and apply them in your life, along with answers to the exercises and reference material.

Now, let's get you started on your path to financial independence!

Part One

BIG DECISIONS FOR DAILY LIVING: HOUSING, TRANSPORTATION, PAYCHECKS, AND TAXES

The planning is done, you've set up your bank accounts, and now it's finally time to move out to your own place. This is an exciting time for sure, but it's full of big financial commitments. If you're like most young adults, you have little or no experience making financial decisions on issues like where to live, when to pay your bills each month, what auto-insurance terms to select, how to file a federal tax return, or who takes all that money out of your paycheck.

Know Your Money

Remember that you are in control of this transition. You want to prove to yourself (and perhaps others) that you can live independently, and you will!

The decisions you make will have either a significant positive impact on your daily life or a significant negative impact, depending on whether they are smart or careless. So no more blaming someone else for your situation. These are your choices, and you'll live with the consequences every day. Now is the time for some educated decision making.

The following chapters will guide you through the key information you'll need to think about *before* you make any financial commitments to successfully navigate this transition to financial independence. All you have to do is know your money. So let's get started, first with housing and transportation and then with paychecks and taxes.

1

APARTMENT BASICS

It's time to move to a place of your own—an exciting transition but also a big financial commitment. Most people rent an apartment before they can afford to own a home. To help you make an informed decision, here are four things to do before you sign a rental or lease agreement:

1. Physically visit the actual unit you will occupy (not a model unit).
2. Consider what you really need in an apartment.
3. Know what you can afford.
4. Know if it's a lease or a rental agreement.

Know Your Money

Housing is usually your biggest expense. For most people, more money goes to pay for housing than anything else. If you get too much house, you will be house rich but cash poor. It's important to live within your means—know what you can afford so you will have money for everything else you need.

Most of the time, you'll sign a lease agreement between you (the tenant) and the landlord or owner. This agreement gives you the right to occupy your new apartment for as long as the lease is in effect—called the *lease term*—in exchange for the periodic payments known as *rent*. A key feature of a lease is a fixed term for tenancy, such as six months or a year; when the time is up, both parties can agree to go their separate ways or renew the lease for another fixed term. The fact that you pay your rent month to month doesn't mean you're automatically off the hook for the remaining payments of the term if you decide to move out early.

By contrast, a *rental agreement* is usually for a short term (such as one month) and automatically renews unless the landlord or tenant decides to end it, which is referred to as *terminating* the agreement. Although this arrangement appears to offer greater flexibility, it may come at a higher price. So before signing anything, be sure you understand the terms of the agreement, evaluate the pros and cons, and determine which option is best for you.

Rent: How Much Can I Afford?

It's easy to fall in love with an expensive apartment and, before you know it, you become house rich but cash poor. Housing is usually your biggest expense, so keeping your rent low will mean you have more money at hand for everything from weekend activities to an emergency car repair. Remember, you don't own it, so it doesn't have to be something you'll love forever. When your lease term is about to expire, find another apartment if a rent increase puts your rent above 28 percent of your income.

Know Your Money

When combined, housing expenses should not exceed 36 percent of what you earn. For rent, spend no more than 28 percent of what you earn. Then add your utilities, renter's insurance, and parking privileges.

One way to have a nicer apartment *and* lower your rent is to find a roommate. A two-bedroom apartment always costs less than two one-bedroom rentals. It's difficult to share your living space with a new person, however, so you'll need to find someone who's easy to get along with, has similar housekeeping habits, and is on the same sleeping schedule. Put the lease agreement in the name of all occupants—meaning your roommates sign the lease with you. That way, you're not stuck with the rent if they can't afford to pay their portion.

Know the rental prices for comparable units in the area before you make a decision. Figure in start-up costs like the following, which can easily add up to as much as three months' rent:

- application fee
- security deposit (one month's rent)
- utility deposits (electricity, gas, cable, phone)
- parking spaces

Don't put these charges on your credit card—you don't want to start out your new life with interest payments.

Visit the Apartment

Showroom models are nice, but you need to visit the actual unit you will be renting so you can visualize your space and ensure that all mechanical systems are operating properly. While there, make sure to do the following checks:

1. Measure the space and make sure your belongings will fit. Include doorways (will your sofa make it through?), closet space, and any shared bathrooms.
2. Locate all cable jacks and electrical outlets.
3. Test the plumbing by turning on faucets (any leaks? hot water?), flushing toilets (turn off properly?), and running the shower (brown water? ample hot water?).

4. Turn on the lights, air-conditioner, heater, and hot-water heater. You may have to arrange for turning on the utilities yourself.
5. Test security, such as doorbells, double front-door locks, windows that close tight and lock, and working fire and carbon-monoxide detectors. How will the landlord respond if a fire alarm goes off or a break-in occurs? Are common hallways and parking lots well lit?
6. Evaluate the neighborhood for noise or smells.
7. Test for Wi-Fi availability and cell phone reception. Watch out for dead zones.

Read the Agreement Thoroughly

Make sure you understand all the terms of your lease or rental agreement before you sign. Afterward, it's usually too late to make a change. Penalties for breaking a lease and a need for cosigners are among the provisions that can cause you trouble.

Breaking Your Lease

Tenants often have good reasons for wanting to end a lease early. If you must break your lease, find out how you can avoid (or minimize) a penalty from your landlord. Some good reasons to discuss are:

- marriage
- called to military duty
- change of job locations
- apartment becomes uninhabitable through no fault of your own (such as crime or natural disaster)
- landlord does not live up to his or her obligations (building repair and maintenance) or invades your privacy (no intervention when neighbors constantly disturb you)

If possible, get any understanding you come to included in the lease, so a change of personnel or memory doesn't undo your agreement down the road.

Cosigners

Landlords may not sign a lease with you if they think you can't pay the rent (for example, if you have no reliable employment or insufficient income at the time of the lease-signing). The landlord may request that you provide someone—a relative or friend— who can cosign the lease as a guarantor. This means if you fail to pay the rent, the cosigner is liable for the amount unpaid even though he or she doesn't live there.

Know Your Money

Until you have ample income to meet your needs, do not cosign a lease for someone else. You do not know the financial maturity of your friend, and you do not want to be burdened with additional payments for a bad situation when your income is limited.

Other Considerations

A lease or rental agreement is a legally binding contract with defined responsibilities. Make sure the lease spells out the details of any of the following that apply:

- your right to use site amenities (such as gym, pool, covered parking)
- proper handling of bedbugs or lead paint before you move in
- whether the agreement is with a broker or the landlord
- money required when you sign the agreement
- return of security deposit
- late payment fees
- pet ownership
- landlord-provided utilities

- interior painting
- what to do when something breaks or needs repair
- subletting rights (roommates)
- penalties for moving out before your lease term is complete
- musical instrument restrictions

Avoid lease terms that automatically renew the agreement for long periods of time (three months or more) or require a ninety-day notice of intent to move out.

There is no guarantee that you and your landlord will agree on things, so give the landlord as much notice as possible (months versus weeks) and keep good records of what you believe justifies your actions, just in case you need to fight a penalty in court. In most cases, you should be okay if you've been a good tenant and the landlord can quickly get another tenant in your apartment.

Renters Insurance

Remember that insurance is about your protection against unforeseeable circumstances. Even if you think, "That can't happen to me," paying for a policy might someday make the difference between an empty apartment and a shopping spree to replace your items. There are many misconceptions about renters insurance, and they can cost you. Consider the following reasons people fail to insure themselves.

"My Landlord Has Me Covered"

In most cases, a landlord's insurance covers only structural damages to the building, and many policies don't cover damage caused by a tenant. If you leave the tub running and it turns your floor into cardboard and dribbles downstairs, damaging your neighbor's couch, you may be liable for the whole drippy mess. If your building burns down, your landlord's insurance will cover repairs but will not replace your personal possessions.

"It's Too Expensive"

Standard coverage includes personal property (for example, up to $40,000), reasonable deductibles (say, $500 per incident), medical coverage for others on the premises, and more. With a higher rate, you can get *replacement cost* coverage, which means that the cost to replace personal items is based on today's cost rather than the older original purchase cost. Raising the deductible lowers your rates.

"I'm in a Great Building and Not Worried about Security"

Renters insurance extends beyond on-premises theft and hazards. If your suitcase is stolen while you're on vacation, or property is stolen from your car, or you hurt someone in your apartment, you will likely be covered.

"My Stuff Isn't Worth Much"

You'd be surprised at how quickly all your things add up. According to "Do I Need Renters Insurance?" on the State Farm website (https://www.statefarm.com/insurance/home-and-property/renters/coverage-options), most people own more than $35,000 worth of property. List each item along with its year of purchase and what you think it would cost to replace today.

"All Insurance Costs the Same"

Insurance rates vary by state, company, and type. Be sure to ask an agent about customizing a policy with more options, and understand what is fully covered or subject to certain limitations. Personal property and natural hazards are particularly prone to limitations you might not expect.

Know Your Money

Get renters insurance. It's a bargain, with many policies under five dollars a month—and it covers your laptop!

Other Common Pitfalls to Avoid

Whether or not you're a first-time renter, avoiding the following common mistakes will help you make a smoother transition.

Failure to Set Housing Priorities

Know your needs versus your wants and stick to them. Which is more important: a gorgeous view or commuting distance? Having access to public transportation or an on-site gym?

No Damage and Repair Inspection

Make sure all damage is noted and repairs are done before you move in. On move-in day, go through the apartment with a pen and paper writing down any defect, no matter how small. Take a picture if you can, date and sign it, and send a copy to your landlord. You don't want to be held liable for preexisting damages.

Forgetting to Figure in the Cost of Basic Items

There are a lot of things you'll need at move-in time to make your place a home you are proud to live in. Make sure you budget for the basics when you set your rent budget:

- furniture—something to sit on, bed and bedding, dresser, lights

- kitchen—basic pans, storage containers, silverware, dishes
- cleaning materials—detergents, broom, dustpan, mop, vacuum cleaner
- bathroom—towels, shower curtain, toiletries
- toolkit—basic tools to hang pictures, assemble things, and install curtains

Discussion

1. What do you need to set up your own apartment? What do you already have?
2. Do you think you have enough stuff to make renters insurance worthwhile?
3. What would happen if you had a lease agreement and your roommate decided not to pay the rent when it's due?
4. What is the role of a cosigner? Should you be a cosigner for someone else?

Conclusion

Before you sign a lease or rental agreement, think about what you really need in your new home, and only make a financial commitment that you can afford. "Know your money" means to live within your means. You can do this by keeping your total housing costs under 36 percent of your income. Don't start out being house rich but cash poor. Your first apartment isn't going to be perfect; you can skip some things for now, and when you earn more income, you can move up to a better apartment.

See appendix 2, "Reference Material," for more information on renters' legal rights.

2

Auto-Insurance Basics

The good news is you finally got a car. The bad news is, now you have an auto-insurance bill to pay too! As you know, driving is not a right—it is a privilege. That's why you need a state driver's license and insurance coverage.

An auto-insurance policy is a contract between you and the insurance company. The company agrees to pay for specific car-related financial losses (specified under the policy terms and conditions) for as long as the policy is in effect in exchange for your periodic payments, called *premiums*. Insurance is usually required by the state you live in and is designed to help the insured vehicle owner pay for losses caused to others. Without this insurance, you risk having to pay the full cost of any harm you cause to others and replacing or repairing your car if it is damaged or stolen.

Know Your Money

To avoid serious future financial hardship, get the proper auto insurance, keep it in effect each year, and don't loan your car to high-risk drivers!

When a vehicle you own causes harm to others, you may be liable for their financial costs, including property damage, medical costs, and legal costs. These costs can easily exceed $100,000 or more, and this even applies when you've loaned your car to someone else who is the one who caused the damage. Without insurance, how will you pay for these obligations? You may have to sell your assets or sacrifice future job earnings.

Each state typically has a minimum level of auto-insurance coverage required by law for vehicle owners. The policy purchase price is directly tied to the risk you represent to the insurance company. In other words, the company determines the likelihood that they're going to have to pay for damages for which you are responsible. Insurance is expensive for young adults under age twenty-five because they cause a lot of damage. Higher risk equals higher policy premiums.

What coverage do you need? No one can predict that, but state law usually requires a minimum level of protection. Ask yourself, how will I pay for damages that exceed my policy limits? As with your apartment agreement, be sure you understand the terms of the insurance policy and evaluate any pros and cons before signing.

Loaning Your Vehicle

If you let your friend borrow your car and he or she crashes it, you will be financially responsible for damages he or she caused even though you weren't driving. You will need to file a claim with your insurance company to pay for the damages, and you will have to pay the deductible that applies. Your future insurance rates may also go up as a result of your claim. If your friend has no auto insurance (referred to as an uninsured motorist) and causes damage that exceeds your policy protection limits, the injured party can come after you for unpaid medical and property-damage costs not paid by your insurance company.

As a general rule, don't loan your vehicle, especially to high-risk drivers. If you loan your car and the borrower causes damage, then you (and your insurance carrier) will pay for the damages. Likewise, if you borrow someone else's vehicle and you cause damage, then that person (and their insurance carrier) will pay for the damages. Lastly, if someone causes damage with your car and you did not give him or her permission to use your car, then that will be handled as car theft.

Standard Coverage and Options

You are covered when the policy lists your name as the insured. The coverage extends to your spouse, other relatives who live in your household, and others who simply have your permission to drive your covered vehicle. If your personal property is in the vehicle when you drive it or when you loan it, usually it is not covered by auto insurance if the vehicle is lost or stolen. It may, however, be covered by your homeowners or renters insurance policy.

Deductibles

A deductible is the portion of a covered financial loss that is your responsibility to pay before the insurance company makes any other payments under your policy. Coverage may be quoted as per incident or per coverage period, such as one year. All coverage is subject to your insurance-policy provisions and applicable endorsements—the terms and conditions. Ask yourself questions like the following:

- How much in out-of-pocket expenses am I willing to pay to get lower premiums?
- Will my own health insurance cover auto-accident injuries?
- Do I have assets to protect, such as investments or future job income?

Know Your Money

A higher deductible will lower the policy premium because the risk of higher payments is transferred from the insurance carrier to you.

Exercise

Deductible and Covered Damages

John's policy deductible is $750. He has a car accident, and the repair shop estimates the cost of repair at $2,000. What will his insurance company pay for covered damages?

See appendix 1, "Exercises," for the answer.

Standard Coverage and Insurance-Carrier Quotes

Your auto-insurance policy is divided into different coverages based on the type of claim that will be paid to you or to others. Typical coverage includes the following three covered events:

1. Bodily injury, per person
2. Bodily injury, per incident
3. Property damage, per incident

Amounts of financial protection for covered activity are called *liability limits*, and they are different for each type of claim. The insurance company may give you a policy quote as "100/300/50," which means you are covered for up to $100,000 protection for bodily injury per person, up to $300,000 bodily injury per incident, and up to $50,000 property protection per incident.

Set your protection limits high enough to protect yourself and your assets against lawsuits for unpaid expenses that exceed your coverage levels. In future years, as your assets and job income increase, so should your insurance coverage.

Standard Options

Generally, you select the terms and conditions that meet your needs. Here is a good list of optional terms you can discuss with your insurance agent to make sure you are getting the best coverage you need and at the best price:

- *Liability coverage*, when an insured motorist is legally responsible, pays for accidental bodily injury and property damage to others. Damages may include medical expenses, pain and suffering, lost wages, and other special damages like legal defense and court costs.
- *Personal Injury Protection (PIP)*, which is required in some states, pays medical expenses for covered persons, regardless of fault, for treatment due to an auto accident. It may also pay for rehabilitation, lost earnings, replacement of services (such as child care), and funeral expenses.
- *Medical payments* take care of medical and funeral expenses for covered persons, regardless of fault, when those expenses are related to an auto accident.
- *Collision* pays for damage to a covered vehicle caused by collision with another object or by upset of the car. A deductible is required.
- *Comprehensive* pays for loss of or damage to a covered vehicle not covered by collision. Examples include loss caused by fire, wind, hail, flood, vandalism, theft, or impact with an animal. A deductible may apply.
- *Uninsured motorist* pays damages when a covered person is injured in an auto accident caused by a driver who does not have liability insurance (this may also include property damage).

- *Underinsured motorist* pays damages when a covered person is injured in an auto accident caused by another driver who has insufficient liability insurance.
- *Rental reimbursement* pays expenses incurred for renting a car when your auto is disabled because of an accident. Daily allowances or limits vary by state and policy provisions.
- *Emergency road service* pays expenses incurred for having your auto towed as a result of a breakdown. Towing limits vary by state and policy provisions.

Savvy Auto-Insurance Shopping

Savvy shopping takes effort and includes calling several carriers and comparing similar coverages and fees, as prices vary widely for the same coverage. Take time to ask questions of an agent, especially regarding various coverage options, how the claims process works, and recent customer satisfaction ratings. And don't forget to ask about premium discounts.

You have the right to change your coverage and policy limits at any time, but your premiums may also change if you do so. Here are some tips you can use to reduce your insurance premiums, although not all will apply for you at the same time:

- Shop around, and do it regularly. Insurance is a competitive industry, and insurers change their rates over time. Make sure you have the best deal you can get each and every year.
- Put multiple vehicles on the same policy. Many insurers offer family discounts.
- If you are covered by your parents' insurance policy, they can assign to you the car that is the least expensive to insure (older and lower in value).
- Get a multiple-policy discount with auto, life, and home from the same carrier.

- Reduce premiums by buying cars with low damage and theft ratings, lower cost to repair, and lower probability of being stolen. Most insurers have their own ratings for these factors.
- Take a defensive-driving course. Insurers offer discounts to drivers who improve their skills.
- Buy vehicles with safety devices like airbags, antilock brakes (ABS), and alarms, because they mitigate theft or the severity of injuries.
- A higher deductible can lower your premium, but balance this with your ability to pay the deductible in the case of an accident.
- Use public transportation or carpooling to reduce your annual mileage.
- Some insurers offer discounts for those with college degrees or in certain professions, such as engineer and teacher.
- Some insurers offer discounts for active or retired members of the military.
- Some insurers offer discounts for purchasing policies online.
- A good driving record with no blemishes gets rewarded.

What to Do in Case of an Accident

Even the most careful drivers may be involved in auto accidents. Knowing what to do after the accident can make the experience less frightening and decrease unnecessary complications. Follow these suggestions:

- Check for injuries. Life and health are more important than damage to vehicles.
- Call the police, even if the accident is minor. Stay at the scene until they arrive. Write down the name of the officer, and provide registration, insurance cards, and accident details.

- Exchange names, addresses, and license information with the other persons involved in the accident. Write down a description of the other vehicles and the accident details (location, time, weather).
- Make note of specific damages to all vehicles involved.
- Jot down names and addresses of witnesses. This will reduce disagreement regarding how the accident actually happened.
- Notify your insurance agent within twenty-four hours (four hours is better).
- Do not sign any document unless it is for the police or your insurance agent.

Tips to Further Reduce the Likelihood of an Accident

- Get more supervised driving education (fifty hours versus ten hours).
- Restrict nighttime driving.
- Avoid aggressive driving habits (tailgating, lane shifts, speeding, rapid braking).
- Limit the number of passengers.
- No using of cell phones or texting when the car is in motion.
- Zero tolerance for drinking and driving. Just don't do it.

Discussion

1. Which coverage is better for you, 100/300/50 or 50/150/50, and why?
2. Are you a better driver when you are alone or when you have several passengers in the car?
3. Do you know someone who has been in a car accident? How did it change him or her?

Conclusion

Driving is a privilege, not a right. As a smart vehicle owner, you must obtain the right auto insurance to both

- ensure the safety of you, your car, and your passengers, and
- safeguard your personal assets from lawsuits.

Young drivers are higher risk because they cause more accidents, so obey the law and avoid speeding, drinking, and texting. Remember, you are financially responsible for damages when you loan your car, so try hard not to do so, especially to high-risk drivers. Shop regularly for the best insurance coverage and fees—premiums can be reduced as you pass age twenty-five and become a safer and more experienced driver.

See appendix 2, "Reference Material," for questions to ask your insurance carrier.

3

PAYCHECKS AND PAYROLL TAXES

For today's young adults, it's a long, long road from high school to a career-related job. But even when you do get a job that pays well, you don't get to keep it all: you must pay taxes. Now it's time to look at your paycheck, taxes, and some new employer-related forms.

Paychecks

A *salary* is a form of compensation for all your efforts over a fixed time period. The payment is usually the same amount each pay period, even though the amount of work produced varies from period to period. A *wage*, on the other hand, is compensation for a fixed task of work and is not tied to a broader time period. Payment is usually for a different amount each pay period, depending on the amount of work produced. When you're hired as a salaried employee, your employer will ask you to provide an IRS tax form W-4 (Employee's Withholding Allowance Certificate). At the end of each calendar year, your employer will provide you with an IRS tax form W-2 (Wage and Tax Statement).

Each payday, you will receive your wages either by cash, check, or direct bank deposit. Your employer defines the pay period, such as the first and fifteenth of the month (twenty-four paydays a year), biweekly (twenty-six paydays a year), or some other arrangement.

Know Your Money

Pay attention to your pay-stub details, and track the changes from pay period to pay period. You will become aware of actual money earned and whether your employer transferred money as you expected. If you have a question, contact your employer right away to discuss your concern.

Take-Home Pay

As you look at your pay stub, you'll notice a big difference between the amount of money you earn—called your *gross* pay—and the smaller amount that you actually get to "take home." Money withheld from you for taxes and other voluntary contributions can easily account for 25 to 35 percent of your salary, leaving you only 65 to 75 percent *net* or *take-home* pay. Regardless of which pay-period term your employer uses, your periodic pay statement will identify the money withheld (either by law or voluntarily) and your total take-home pay.

Commonly Used Terms

You may see the following terms on your pay stub:

- *Gross wages* are earnings before any withholding (tax or voluntary).
- *Withholding* is money earned but not received. Your employer deducts these funds and submits payment on your behalf.
- *Net wages* are earnings after withholding (take-home pay).
- *Exemptions* are the number of dependents under your personal financial care.

Withholding

Each employer may have any of the following items withheld each pay period:

- federal income tax (FIT)
- Federal Insurance Contributions Act (FICA), also known as social-security tax; two components are Medicare and OASDI (Old Age, Survivors, and Disability Insurance)
- state income tax (SIT)
- state disability insurance (SDI) and unemployment insurance (SUI)
- local taxes
- voluntary contributions to retirement plans, such as 401(k)s
- voluntary contributions to flexible-spending accounts (FSA)

Exercise

Take-Home Pay

What percentage of your gross salary do you receive as take-home pay, for the pay period and for the year, given the following details?

- salary per pay period: $1,540
- federal tax rate (all items): 25 percent
- retirement-plan account: $75 per pay period
- pay-period frequency: biweekly
- state tax rate (all items): 2.5 percent
- flexible-spending account: $150 per pay period

See appendix 1, "Exercises," for the answer.

Payroll Taxes

Federal and state governments have the power to tax people's income through approved tax legislation. There are various kinds of taxes, such as income, investment, estate, and sales. Some taxes, such as sales tax, are paid on each transaction; others, such as income tax, are paid annually. For payroll taxes, the employer deducts an amount from your earned income each pay period based on the amount you earned and submits the money to the government on your behalf. Withholding a little bit throughout the year is easier than paying a big lump sum at a time when you may not have that money anymore. You may even get a refund. The more you earn, the more your employer deducts.

The federal government enforces the tax code through the Internal Revenue Service (IRS) by combining information from many sources to verify that the tax information you submit correctly matches the amount owed.

Wage and Tax Statement (Form W-2)

After each calendar year, employers are required to provide W-2 information to both the employee and the IRS. People who work for more than one company will have a W-2 form from each employer. Employees are to include all W-2 information as part of their personal tax returns. The W-2 statement must show:

- income earned, including all wages (such as cash and tips) and other noncash compensation, and
- taxes, including income taxes, withheld from the money paid to the employee.

Employee's Withholding Allowance Certificate (Form W-4)

This certificate provides employers with your filing status and number of exemptions (people you are financially responsible for) so they can withhold the correct amount of money from your paycheck. The higher the number of exemptions, the lower the total money withheld and vice versa. If you withhold too much, you give Uncle Sam your money with no interest throughout the year; if you withhold too little, you will pay with additional cash when you file your taxes, whether you still have that money or not.

Your exemption options are as follows:

- *Single* means you are claiming only yourself. If Form W-4 fails to show that an employee is married, the employer must withhold according to the single employee tables.
- *Married* means you are claiming yourself and a spouse. Married employees must indicate their status on Form W-4 to take advantage of the lower withholding.
- *Head of household* means you are unmarried but pay more than 50 percent of the cost of keeping up a home for yourself and one or more of your dependents or other qualifying individuals. Persons claiming head-of-household status are to complete Form W-4 as "single."

Payroll Tax Withholding: Federal

Throughout the year, employers collect your tax payments by withholding various amounts from your earned income each pay period. The amount to be withheld is established by law and subject to change. To see the current tax tables go to www.irs.gov.

FICA defines tax rates to be paid and used to fund two federal programs: OASDI (commonly referred to as Social Security) and Medicare. The employer and the employee each pay a portion of the tax for Medicare and OASDI.

The Federal Unemployment Tax Act (FUTA) defines tax rates to be paid and used to fund federal workforce agencies (various job-development and service programs) and one-half of the cost of extended unemployment benefits.

Payroll Tax Withholding: State and Local

Most states rely on the federal income-tax form to provide the basis for state taxation. Many states also tax your income to pay for disability and unemployment insurance. Some cities add a local payroll tax as well; ask your employer for details.

Discussion

1. Should your personal budget be based on your gross earnings or your take-home pay?
2. How can withholdings enhance your financial future?
3. Is it better to withhold

   - a lower amount throughout the year and, when you file your tax returns, pay additional money, or
   - a higher amount throughout the year and, when you file your tax returns, pay no additional money?

Conclusion

Payroll taxes are an obligation, but proper withholding will help you avoid a big tax bill when you file your income tax return by April 15. Be aware of the changes in the tax code each year, and change your withholding (W-4 exemptions, voluntary items) as factors in your life change. See appendix 2, "Reference Material," for further paycheck and payroll details.

4

FEDERAL TAX-FILING BASICS

Disclaimer: This brief review of Form 1040, the US Individual Income Tax Return, is not intended to provide readers with any tax advice regarding their unique tax situation, but rather to introduce young adults to collecting the information needed to complete a tax return. Please consult with a tax expert to review your individual tax situation and receive advice on any tax-related matters.

Form 1040: Component Overview

IRS Form 1040 relies on information that ultimately establishes your tax liability and any balance due, whether payment or refund. Because there are so many tax laws and supporting documents, we will limit our focus to the basic categories of information needed to complete the form.

Form 1040EZ is the simplest of the three 1040 tax forms. If your taxable income is less than $100,000, you don't claim any dependents, you file as single or married filing jointly, and you have interest income less than $1,500, you may be eligible to file Form 1040EZ. The one-page form has four short sections to complete. If you don't qualify for this simple form, use Form

1040, which is more detailed but may also result in a lower tax obligation.

Note that the taxable period is a calendar year—that is, January 1 through December 31—even though the federal government budgets and operates on a fiscal year that starts on October 1 and ends on September 30. Let's start looking into the reporting process.

Personal Information

You'll need to provide your name, address, social-security number, filing status, and exemptions. Your filing status (such as single or married filing jointly) is used to determine your filing requirements, standard deduction, eligibility for certain credits, and correct tax. If more than one filing status applies to you, choose the one that will result in the lowest amount of tax.

Income

You'll need to provide information regarding *all* your sources of income. In addition to a salary or wages, other income sources include investments (interest, dividends, sales), alimony, business (if self-employed), retirement (IRA, pension), government (social security, unemployment), or other (legal settlements, tips). The common IRS forms listing income are:

- Form W-2 (salary or wages)
- Form 1099 (interest, dividends, consulting work, retirement)
- Schedule K-1 (business ownership)
- Form 8949 (asset sale)

However, you must report all income (such as tips), even if you did not receive an appropriate form. Add them all to calculate your total income.

Next, the tax code allows you to adjust your income downward for various reasons that change from time to time by law. Adjustments are for expenses related to activities the government wants to promote, such as education (tuition, fees, student-loan interest), business (if self-employed), alimony, health savings accounts, IRAs, or moving to a new home. Add them all up and then subtract the sum from your total income to determine your adjusted gross income (AGI).

Deductions, Exemptions, and Credits

Three more ways the government allows you to adjust your income downward are deductions, exemptions, and credits:

- *Deductions* include expenses for medical, state, and local taxes; interest paid on loans (such as a mortgage); donations to charity; and job-hunting expenses. For tax purposes, you have an option to select a standard value set by the tax code, or you can provide information regarding the actual money you spent, which is called *itemizing your deductions.* Schedules A, B, and C are some of the forms you'll need for this.
- *Exemptions* are an allowance—a fixed dollar amount— tied to your number of dependents.
- *Credits* are allowances for specific activities, such as education, residential energy, retirement savings, and foreign taxes paid.

Companies will send you tax-related forms and information before the end of February, so be sure to keep them for future reference. Common IRS forms for this purpose are 1098, which lists the amount you paid in mortgage interest; 1098-T, which documents tuition paid; and 1098-E, which lists student loan interest.

Add all your deductions, exemptions, and credits together to determine your total tax and credits, and then subtract that sum from your AGI to calculate your taxable income.

Taxes Due, Balance Due

Now that you know your taxable income, you can determine how much tax you owe and must pay for the year. The IRS publishes tax tables that change annually, and these tables help you look up how much you owe. You can locate your taxable income in the tax table and see the tax amount due, or you can calculate the tax (see appendix 2, "Reference Material"). Be sure to use the tax information tied to your filing status—such as single or married filing jointly—because the taxes will be different.

Tax Withholding and Taxes Owed

Each tax form that reports your income (such as W-2 or 1099) also lists how much money was withheld from your income for federal taxes. If the number is zero or the box is blank, then nothing was withheld. Any amount listed was previously submitted to the government on your behalf by your income provider, tied to your social-security number or other tax-identification number. Add all your various amounts together to determine your total tax withholding. Note that the tax forms also list any withholding for state and local tax purposes. You should use this information when preparing your state tax return.

Form 1040 compares your total tax withholding to your tax bill, and the difference will tell you whether you must make an additional payment (not enough withholding) or if you should expect a refund (too much withholding, and the government returns your money).

Filing Your Tax Return

To file an individual return, taxpayers can download forms and instructions online at http://www.irs.gov, print them out, fill them out, and mail them in. You don't have to use the paper version, though; the IRS also allows you to e-file online. The system will automatically decide which Form 1040 you need.

More than 80 percent of taxpayers use IRS e-file, which you can learn more about at http://www.irs.gov/Filing.

Form 1040, all supporting forms (like W-2 and schedules), and any tax payments must be filed each year no later than April 15 for the previous year. If that date falls on a weekend, the deadline is extended to the following Monday. Filing can be done by mail (postmarked by midnight) or online (showing a submission time before midnight). Your submitted form is not complete unless it is signed with a written or electronic signature. If it is not, the IRS will not accept the form for processing.

Taxpayers due a refund can select to receive the money by check or electronic funds transfer to a bank account. The latter gets your money to you much more quickly—about ten days as opposed to several months.

If you need more time to collect the information necessary to complete your tax return, you can file for an extension (using Form 4869 for individual income tax returns) no later than April 15. Although this grants you up to six months to complete and file your return, you must submit an estimated tax payment if you think an additional amount is owed. Once you file your Form 1040, there will be penalty fees if you owe an additional amount beyond what was estimated on your extension application.

Know Your Money

Taxpayers are entitled to take all lawful steps to minimize their tax liability—for example, by claiming valid charitable contributions. Filing a tax return with false information, however, is a crime punishable by law, known as tax evasion.

Common Tax Mistakes to Avoid

Mistakes can delay the processing of your return and mailing of your refund. They can also lead to more serious problems, such as an IRS audit. Proofread your return to avoid potential issues. According to the IRS, the following are some of the most common errors made on income-tax returns:

- *Name is wrong or misspelled.*
- *Social-security number is incorrect.*
- *Taxpayer fails to file a return.* Even if you don't owe taxes, you must still file a return. Taxpayers forfeit refunds if they don't file returns within three years.
- *The wrong IRS form is used.*
- *Taxpayer makes math errors when filling out paper form.* This is an advantage of online filing—software programs do the math for you.
- *Return is unsigned and undated.* If you're filing as married, both must sign and date. If you e-file your return, you must sign electronically using your PIN, your AGI from the prior year return's, and your birth date—and all data must be correct
- *Income not included on a W-2 or 1099 is left off return.*
- *Bank account number for direct deposit is incorrect.* While direct deposit is a fast and safe way to receive a refund, it can't happen if there are errors in the routing and account numbers you've entered.
- *Payroll taxes for people you hire are unpaid and unreported.* Paying the nanny under the table can come back to haunt you.
- *The wrong filing status is checked.* Taxpayers often incorrectly claim head-of-household status without meeting the requirements.
- *Credits and deductions are figured incorrectly.* This is especially a problem with the earned income credit

and standard deductions. A deduction can be a child or relative but never a spouse.

- *Low- to moderate-income individuals overlook the earned income credit.* If you meet the requirements, take the credit.
- *Taxpayer forgets about the alternative minimum tax.* This tax is an attempt by the IRS to ensure that anyone who benefits from these tax advantages pays at least a minimum amount of tax according to the government

---

Exercise

Tax Calculation

Using the tax formulas in appendix 2, "Reference Material," what is your total tax bill—that is, how much tax you owe—given the following information? What does your Form 1040 show as the refund or amount you owe?

Total income: $56,600
Tuition and fees: $6,000
Exemptions (1): $ 3,900
Standard deduction: $6,100

Filing status: single
Student-loan interest: $1,800
Dependents: none
Withholding: $6,392.50

Fill in the missing information:

Total income	$
Tuition and fees	$
Student-loan interest	$
AGI	$
Standard deduction	$
Exemptions	$
Taxable income	$
Total tax bill	$
Total tax withholding	$
Balance due (amount you owe/refund)	$

See appendix 1, "Exercises," for the answer.

Discussion

1. Who sets the rules for US taxpayers?
2. Who enforces them?
3. How often do the rules change?
4. Compare your taxable income and your tax rate. What happens to the tax rate as the taxable income gets larger? Is this fair?

Conclusion

Each calendar year, most US residents with earned income must pay taxes to the US government and are required to file a federal tax return (US Individual Income Tax Return, commonly known as Form 1040). You must file by April 15 of the following year. You must file a return even if you do not owe any tax. The government enforces the tax code through the IRS by combining information from many sources to verify that the tax information you submit correctly matches the amount owed. All taxpayers are entitled to take all lawful steps to minimize their tax liability, like claiming deductions and credits. Filing a tax return with false information is a crime punishable by law, known as tax evasion.

See appendix 2, "Reference Material," for more information.

5

Paying Bills: Online and on Paper

There are many reasons people don't pay their bills on time: lack of organization, poor budgeting skills, misplaced bills, even simple procrastination. Paying bills late is very expensive, however, especially for credit cards. Fees for late payments are often ten to forty dollars for each credit card, and interest rates can skyrocket to 25 percent or more. Who wants that? Fortunately, it's easy to avoid the fees, higher interest rates, and negative dings on your credit report.

Rather than sporadically paying your bills as they come in or checking a pile on your desk every few days, set aside an hour twice a month for paying your bills. You can pay the old-fashioned way with checks and stamps or go more tech-savvy with software programs and online services. However you do it, the first step is to get organized.

Setup

The following setup activities help lay the foundation for good bill-paying organization:

1. Make a list of all your bills for an entire year. If you do not know the actual cost of some bills, use your best estimate. Note which ones are paid regularly versus nonregularly.

   a. *Regularly* means the same amount and frequency each month, such as a monthly student loan payment or cable TV bill. Add these all up and divide by twelve to determine how much money to set aside each month.

   b. *Nonregularly* means the bills have different amounts and frequency, as with clothing expenses, car insurance, credit-card bills, and cell-phone charges. Add them all up and divide by twelve to determine how much money to set aside each month.

2. Identify how often your employer pays you. Is it twice a month, every two weeks, or once a month?

3. Create a separate checking account devoted to bill paying. Divide the amount of money to be set aside each month by the number of pay periods. This is the amount of money you should transfer into your checking account every pay period. The other money should be kept in a different account, such as emergency or regular savings. (*Tip:* Keep an emergency savings account in case of disaster. This should include one month's expenses plus insurance deductibles. For example, if your car insurance policy has a $1,000 deductible, then keep $1,000 in your emergency account just in case you have a car accident.)

4. Create a separate e-mail address just for electronic bills and various statements (such as bank or investment) so you never lose your bills in your regular e-mail.

5. Create a bill-paying station to be your one dedicated place for all your bills. It can be a small shelf or an even a basket.

Bills and Statements

With the basic foundation in place, move on to the following process for organizing your bills and statements as they come in:

1. Open your bills immediately when you receive them by mail or e-mail.
2. For paper mail, use a red pen to write the due date and the amount owed on the front of each envelope. Pay close attention, as due dates are not always the same each month.
3. For e-mail, create a folder for each month. Forward and file each e-mail notice to the right folder and change the subject line to the following information: entity owed, due date, amount due. For example: "PSE&G Gas, 4-28-2013, $56.00."
4. Highlight any charges or parts of your bill that you question. You'll follow up on these issues later.
5. Throw away any envelope stuffers that don't include personal information, such as special offers or promotions for other products.
6. Shred any paper that includes personal information. Don't ever throw those away—it puts your financial information at risk. If you don't have a shredder, many office-supply stores offer access to shredders for a nominal fee.
7. Place all your paper unpaid bills in one folder for future reference. Do not put your utility bill in one folder, student loan in another. All pending bills should be together—it's faster, easier, and more efficient.
8. Place all your statements in a folder labeled for the month due and file it in your filing system.

Paying the Bills: When and How

Next, follow these steps to link your bill-paying activity to your employer's payday so you can always pay your bills on time.

1. Decide on the two days per month when you will pay your bills. Block off one hour of your time on the calendar, just as you would any other appointment. Most people choose days tied to the days they get paid. If you get paid twice a month on the first and fifteenth, then you would decide to pay bills on the seventh and twenty-second of each month. This gives you one week to iron out any paycheck problems that may arise before you actually pay your bills.

2. Organize your bills by due date in both your paper and electronic folders. Allow about one week for payments to arrive through the mail system.

   • On the seventh of each month, pay bills that are due between the sixteenth and the thirty-first.

   • On the twenty-second of each month, pay bills that are due between the first and the fifteenth.

3. Balance your bill payments for each period. If you are depositing $1,000 each pay period, then you want to pay as close to $1,000 as you can. If the amount due exceeds the deposit, you'll need to make adjustments, such as the following:

   • Defer payments that have no due date, such as deposits to savings, to the following pay period.

   • Contact companies to negotiate a new billing date later in the month.

   • Pay essential bills first (rent, groceries, utilities, things that allow you to work) and nonessentials later (Internet, cable, clothes).

   • Pay highest interest-rate debt first and then lower interest-rate debt.

- Take advantage of promotional offers

- Pay 50 percent early in the month and 50 percent later in the month.

4. For each paper bill, write a check, record the transaction in your check register, put the check into the return envelope provided along with the part of the bill indicated for return, stamp the envelope, and mail the envelope.
5. Create a master list of all payments (either check or online). Write the company name, date, amount paid, and check number for future reference. For online payments, note any confirmation numbers.
6. Review your online accounts for accuracy. If you've highlighted any problems with your bill or your statement, now is the time to call and solve the problem. If you can't reach anyone, add this task to the next day, noting your account number, customer-service phone numbers, and specific question.
7. If any of these bills are needed for tax purposes, file it with your yearly tax documents.
8. When done paying bills, place your master list of all payments and any paper copies into an envelope labeled for that month and file it in your filing system.

Know Your Money

When it comes time to get rid of old bank or financial records, it's never a good idea to just throw them in the trash. These types of documents can easily be used to steal your identity. Shred them instead.

Online Bill Pay

Paying bills online is becoming very popular with today's young adults. It keeps them organized in a technology-centric way, it eliminates errors, and it saves time. The primary advantages are convenience and control. Eliminate the hassle of writing checks or having multiple billing sites with multiple passwords. Simply sign in, enter who to pay, enter the amount and date, and submit—it's that easy. You determine when payments are made and for how much while maintaining the ability to update or cancel payments before they are processed. And it is usually free.

These online systems are provided by banks and Internet service companies (like http://www.manilla.com), and you can choose to input things manually each month or sign up for automatic transactions. The primary advantages are convenience and control.

Know Your Money

Be aware that automatic payments will be withdrawn from your account even if you don't have enough money to cover the payment. Ouch—here come the fees and credit-report problems!

Because you will be sharing your personal financial information, be sure to protect it.

- Websites—be sure the website is secure. The web address should start with "https," and there should be a padlock icon somewhere on the browser window.
- Passwords—be sure to use "tough" passwords. They should include letters, numbers, and symbols. You should change them often (i.e., sixty days) or when needed (i.e., bank notice of potential problem).

Start out by paying your bills online on a case-by-case basis, especially if the payment value changes each month. Once you are comfortable that the site works well, you can migrate to automatic payments, at least for those regular bills for which the amount stays the same.

Additional financial protection is available when you use a credit card instead of a debit card. You can legally withhold payment to a credit-card issuer for suspected fraudulent charges until the issue is resolved. With debit cards, which are linked to your accounts, once your money is gone it is very hard to recover.

Discussion

1. Do you think paying bills online is safer than paying by check? Why or why not?
2. What happens if you do not keep your "bills to be paid" well organized?
3. How strong are your passwords?

Conclusion

Paying bills late becomes very expensive, especially for credit cards, so the most important thing is to find a system that works for you. The basics of keeping your bills organized boils down to keeping them in one place and paying them according to a set schedule. If you use online bill-payment methods, be sure the website is secure, you use tough passwords (with letters, numbers, and symbols), and you stay on top of authorized automatic payments. Don't throw old bank or financial records in the trash, because paper documents can easily be used to steal your identity. Shred them instead. Finally, it's a good idea to save select documents to support your tax returns. You have three years to file an amended tax return, so keep your documentation for three years, in case the IRS decides to audit you.

Part Two

PROTECT YOUR MONEY: CHECKING, CREDIT AND DEBIT CARDS, AND CREDIT SCORE

Whether you need to get more money by borrowing or have some extra money on hand to invest and save, there are a lot of companies to work with and a lot of service options to help you. You may be wondering if you need a relationship with a bank anymore, what different services there are to choose from, and which one is best for you.

The following chapters will guide you through the key information you need to think about *before* you open an account and help you successfully navigate this transition to financial independence. All you have to do is know your money. So let's get started—first with checking accounts, then with credit and debit cards, and finally with your credit score and protecting your financial information.

6

CHECKING-ACCOUNT BASICS

Today's generation of young adults is less interested in using checking accounts the traditional way, by physically writing checks. They prefer online banking and debit cards. However, checking accounts remain an important form of credit, and there are times when you really do need to write a check. Most banks offer checking accounts plus ATMs (automatic teller machines) and electronic funds-transfer services. They also charge you service fees in a variety of ways (such as per-check charge, minimum balances, ATM fees), so you need to know how to avoid or minimize these fees.

When you write a check, you are giving permission (via your signature) to a person or organization to submit the check for payment to their bank. Their bank will process the check, and ultimately the money will be drawn from your account, so you'd better have the money in your account to cover the check's value.

If not enough money is in the account, the check will bounce (banks call it an *overdraft*). This means that the bank will not pay it, and you will be charged a service fee. Banks and industry watchdogs keep track of how people use their checking accounts. If you bounce too many checks, your bank will likely close your account, and this will hurt your credit score. So keep your credit record clean by using checking accounts properly. Store your checks in a safe place, and if you lose any, be sure to notify your bank immediately to stop payment on those checks.

Know Your Money

Bounced checks are considered a key predictor of future credit problems and put you in a higher risk category. So keep your credit record clean by using checking accounts properly!

Check Features

Checks are preprinted with many features to help you and the bank keep track of your checks and your account. They include the following:

- decorative paper, usually featuring a pattern or picture
- account name (your name), check number, bank name (your bank)
- formatted spaces to enter the date, who you're writing the check to, how much it's for, your signature, and a memo to remind you of the purpose of the check.
- MICR code, a fixed-format number that allows the depositor's bank to route the check to the payer's bank and identify from which customer account the funds are to be drawn. The fixed format includes the

    ○ transit routing number (also known as the ABA number), nine digits that identify the Federal Reserve district and branch responsible for handling the issuing bank activity, an availability classification, issuing bank number, and check digit;
    ○ payer's account number, fourteen digits assigned to the payer by the issuing bank;

○ serial number, usually the check number (same as top right corner number), which is key for processing any stop-payment requests; and

○ encoded amount of the check, which is not preprinted but printed during the processing of the check.

Exercise

Identify Check Features

Find the MICR code information preprinted on your checks. What is your bank's nine-digit ABA number? Can you also identify your account number and check number?

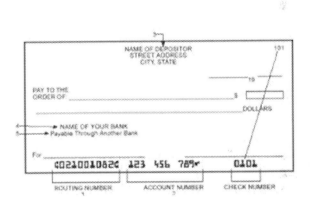

How to Write a Check

Follow these steps to make out your check:

1. Use ink, never a pencil. Pencil can be erased, and someone could maliciously alter the information.
2. Enter the date.
3. On the line labeled "Pay to the Order of," write the name of the person, business, or organization you want to receive the money.

4. On the right-hand side is a line labeled "$_____." Write the numerical value of the money to be given in the format of dollars and cents (for example, "$125.23").

5. Below the "Pay to the Order of" line, write the spelled out (alphabetic) value of the money to be paid (for example, "One Hundred Twenty Five and 23/100 dollars").

6. Make sure the numerical and the spelled-out amount match. If they don't, usually the spelled-out amount is paid and the bank may charge you a fee.

7. On the line labeled "Memo," you can insert any notation you want (for example, "Happy Birthday Gift"), but it's okay to leave it blank.

8. In the bottom right corner is a line for your signature. You should have a consistent signature (the same on all checks) to help the bank spot fraud. Remember, your check is not legal until you sign it.

Some additional tips:

- Don't leave any blank spaces in the key writing areas, and write legibly.
- If you need cash, you can write yourself a check—just write "CASH" on the "Pay to the Order of" line. However, if you lose this check, anyone can present it to a bank and get the money. It is better to write the check to cash when you are in your bank and can sign it in the presence of a bank teller.
- Once you have written the check, record the check number, date, who the check was made out to, and amount in your check register.
- If you make a mistake, write "VOID" across the face of the check in big letters so no one can use it. In the check register, record a $0 value for that check number.

Know Your Money

Poor use of your checking account hurts your credit rating, as bounced checks are considered a key predictor of future credit problems. So keep your credit record clean by using your checking account properly, storing your checks in a safe place, and notifying your bank immediately if you lose them.

Check Endorsements

When you receive a check from someone else, you can deposit the check at your bank to get the money or sign it over to someone else to give them the money. These instructions are called your *endorsement*. You write your endorsement on the back of the check in the section labeled "Endorse Here." Sign your name exactly as it appears on the "Pay to the Order of " line on the front of the check, even if it isn't spelled correctly. Then sign again with the correct spelling if necessary. The following are the most common types of endorsements:

- A *blank endorsement* is simply your signature—your name only.
- A *restrictive endorsement* is safer and recommended, especially if you're mailing your check or someone else is depositing your check for you into your account. In this case, in addition to your signature, you would write, "For deposit only" and your account number.
- A *special endorsement* gives the money to someone else. Write the person's name—for example, "Pay to the Order of John Smith"—and then add your signature.

Check-Clearing Process

The national check-clearing system is called ACH (automatic clearinghouse). This is where the bank of the depositor contacts the payer's bank for payment, and the money is transferred from the payer's bank to the depositor's bank. Computers read the MICR code on the bottom of the check to locate the paying bank and the payer's checking account number and the funds— the written value of the check—are deducted from the payer's checking account in one or two days.

When there's not enough money in the payer's account, the check will not be paid—it will bounce. If it's later resubmitted and the funds are available, it will be paid, or "clear the account." Every time a check bounces, the bank charges you a fee (often ten dollars or more).

The Check Clearing for the 21st Century Act (Check 21) was signed into law and became effective in 2004. Instead of physically moving paper checks from one bank to another, banks can now transmit data electronically by capturing a picture of the front and back of the check along with the associated payment information. If necessary, banks can create a paper substitute check from the electronic image.

Balancing Your Checkbook

Being financially responsible for your checking account means you should know about how much money is in your account so you don't write a check for more money than you have. This will prevent bounced checks and fees, and improve your credit score.

The list you keep with your checkbook that contains information from all the checks you write and all the deposits you give the bank is called the *check register*. This lets you know how much money is in your account at any point in time. When your monthly bank statement arrives, you compare the money noted on your statement (the actual money in your account) with your check register (what you think is in your account). This is called *balancing your checkbook*. See the detailed process in the exercise below.

Sometimes you may find a check that cleared the bank but you forgot to write it in the register, so you have less money in your account than you thought you did. On the other hand, you may find a deposit you gave the bank but forgot to write in the register—in that much more pleasant case, you have more money in your account than you expected. Checking accounts provide excellent financial flexibility, but to use them safely, you must be responsible for your spending behavior and balance your checkbook regularly.

Exercise

Balance Your Checkbook
Using your check register:

1. Check off each withdrawal that is listed in your bank statement.
2. On a separate piece of paper, write your check register ending balance.
3. List any interest earned (if you have an interest-bearing account), automatic deposits, overdraft line of credit, or other electronic deposits not previously recorded but listed on your bank statement. Add up these items.
4. Subtract any service charges, automatic payments, transfers, or other electronic withdrawals not previously recorded but listed on your bank statement. Add up these items.
5. Add lines 2 and 3 and subtract line 4 for your *adjusted check register*.
6. Using your bank statement:
7. On a separate piece of paper, write your bank statement ending balance.
8. List the deposits from your check register that do not appear on the bank statement. Add up these items.
9. List the withdrawals from your check register that do not appear on the bank statement. Add up these items.

10. Add lines 1 and 2 and then subtract line 3 for your *adjusted bank statement.*

Compare your adjusted check register to your adjusted bank statement. If the numbers are equal, congratulations! You balanced your checkbook. If they're not equal, review your register for math errors, and look for additional items in your check register that were not "checked off" from your bank statement. Repeat the entire process until the adjusted amounts are equal.

Using Your Money

Bank accounts help you keep your money secure. In addition to checks, you should know these other ways of accessing and transferring your money.

Automatic Teller Machines (ATM)

Banks will often give you a debit card that is linked to your checking account. To get cash from your account, you can use this card for ATM transactions. At an ATM, you enter your card and PIN (personal identification number) and tell the machine how much cash you want to withdraw. Often, banks charge you a fee every time you use an ATM.

Debit cards are different from credit cards because you don't get a bill at the end of the month to pay. Rather, each time you use the card (such as at an ATM), a message is sent to your bank to approve the transaction—that is, verify you have enough money in your account. Once approved, the money is instantly taken out of your account, and the cash is then released from the ATM.

Electronic Funds Transfer (EFT)

Banks offer a service of transferring money from one bank account to another without any paper money changing hands. The bank uses the ACH network to connect with other financial institutions. Using the funds-transfer information from your checking account—the MICR code discussed above under "Check Features"—financial institutions can process electronic transactions for a variety of purposes, such as deposits (including direct-deposit paychecks from your employer) or payments (like your car loan that's due every month). The different types of money transfers include personal or business checks, ATMs, credit-card purchases, and wire transfers.

Discussion

1. What does it mean to "balance your checkbook"? How often should you do this?
2. Why is it a good idea to know what money is in your checking account at all times?
3. What happens to your credit score if you use the checking account properly? If you don't?
4. Do you really need a checking account?
5. Is it easier to write paper checks or to use online banking tools?

Conclusion

Checking accounts are a convenient way to exchange funds with others, whether you're paying bills or accepting deposits. Poor use of a checking account hurts your credit rating, as bounced checks are considered a key predictor of future credit problems. Store your checks in a safe place, and if you lose them, notify your bank immediately. Knowing your money means regularly balancing your checkbook. It's easy to do, and when you can explain the difference between your check register and your bank statement at the end of the month, then your account is in balance.

7

CREDIT-CARD BASICS

We all need to start somewhere. Establishing credit for yourself can be challenging because you have no history of being creditworthy or having a long-term income. In this economic environment, lenders are being extra cautious about extending credit. They want to do everything in their power to take on as little risk as possible, so those with the best credit histories and highest scores will get the best deals. President Obama signed a law whereby credit-card issuers are banned from issuing cards to anyone under twenty-one without an adult cosigner or proof that the young person has enough income to pay the bill.

According to a 2009 survey conducted by Sallie Mae, 91 percent of college undergraduates have a credit card. In 2008, the average credit-card debt of all college students was $3,173, with freshmen averaging $2,038 and seniors averaging $4,138. Combine this debt with student loans and a tough postgraduation job market, and the result is a tough start to becoming financially independent.

Know Your Money

Create a solid, clean credit history for yourself with a good credit score. Whatever kind of card you start out with, you have it in your power to succeed if you never charge more than you can pay, and then pay in full so you don't face interest charges. When you can't pay in full, make sure to pay on time so there are no late fees.

Getting Started

Before you apply for credit, it's smart to make sure no one else has fraudulently tried to use your name or social-security number to obtain credit. Do this by checking your credit reports for free at http://www.annualcreditreport.com. Next, go shopping for a credit card and decide which one is best for you. There are thousands to choose from. Look for a card with the lowest possible interest rate and no annual fee.

Finally, open up a checking and/or savings account with your local bank if you haven't done so already. Even if your account doesn't have a lot of money in it or you don't use it often, lenders still see these accounts as a sign of your financial responsibility.

Choose the Right Credit Card for You

There are many card options, but several are unattractive, so when shopping for your cards keep these general guidelines in mind. The two most important factors in choosing credit cards wisely are your knowledge of the terms upon which any card is offered to you and your own habits and patterns of use. What constitutes the best card for you depends entirely on how you use your credit. Ask yourself three key questions:

1. *Do I tend to carry a balance?* If the answer is yes, look for cards with low interest rates—and a guaranteed fixed low interest rate, even with an annual fee, if you know you'll be carrying that balance for a long time.

2. *Do I pay my balance in full most of the time?* If you do, the interest rate a card charges may be of less concern to you than the benefits it offers. Extra warranty protection may be very important to a person who frequently uses a credit card to purchase valuable electronic or computer equipment, while someone who travels often might value the traveler's accident insurance another card offers.

3. *What rebate programs appeal to me?* An auto rebate might be very appealing to an individual saving to purchase a new car, whereas airline miles would be the rebate of choice for the globetrotter looking to squeeze in one more trip this year. If a rebate program is likely to give you a return that is truly useful to you, it's probably worth signing up, even though these cards often have an annual fee.

Once you have identified what you really want and need in a card, it's time to start paying attention to the specific terms for each card you have or are offered. The trick is to find the card with the features and costs that fit your use patterns.

Know Your Money

Credit-card numbers explained, for the inner math nerd in you: Credit-card numbers follow the Luhn formula, a simple checksum formula used to verify that a credit-card number is valid. Start from the right and double each second digit (for example 1111 becomes 2121); if the doubling creates a two-digit number, add those digits together. Then add all the digits together. A valid credit-card number should result in a sum evenly divisible by ten.

Read the Small Print

By carefully reading the terms of each credit-card agreement, you can ensure that the card or cards you've chosen for your credit needs will serve you well and in a cost-effective manner. The important thing is to be sure that you understand how the card works and what you can expect as a credit-active consumer using that card. Here are some questions to ask:

- What is the interest rate, and is it fixed or variable? If it is a special low-interest offer, how long will the low rate apply and to what kind of transactions?
- How is interest calculated? Some card agreements base interest on the average daily balance from the past cycle, while others use a two-cycle method and base interest on purchases from the past two months.
- Is there a grace period before interest is charged? If so, how long is it?
- What is the annual fee, if any?
- What other fees may be imposed and under what circumstances? Many card issuers are charging higher late and over-the-limit fees than in the past, to encourage customers to be more responsible about their credit accounts. If you're sometimes absentminded, a card with great interest rates but high fees might not be cost-effective for you.
- What special features or programs does this card offer? Will you be taking advantage of them?

There's no one right card for everybody, so make sure you've chosen the one that fits you. Read the terms carefully along with any notices you receive of changes to your agreement.

Interest Rate versus Annual Percentage Rate (APR)

The interest rate is the percentage of the loan amount that is charged for borrowing the money. The annual percentage rate (APR) is the percentage of the loan amount that is charged for borrowing the money plus any lender fees. The idea behind the APR is to help consumers understand the difference between the fees and interest charges (i.e., higher fees and lower interest rate or lower fees and higher interest rate).

The federal Truth In Lending Act requires companies to show the APR next to the interest rate. The APR percentage is usually higher than the interest rate because it includes the lender fees.

Credit card interest rates can range from 0 percent to 30 percent. To determine what interest rate companies will charge you, they consider a variety of factors, such as your credit score, income, assets, debt-payment history, credit limit (total amount you can borrow at one time), grace period (extra days to make a payment without penalty even though it is late), and more.

The lowest credit card interest rates and lender fees are offered to consumers with a strong credit history. It's often hard to get your first credit card (i.e., no credit history), and it gets easier over the coming years.

Actual interest charges are usually calculated by multiplying the daily account balance by the periodic rate (the APR rate divided by the number of days in a year).

Universal Default

Beware! Look carefully for this phrase in your credit-card terms. Universal default allows credit-card issuers to increase interest rates at any time, for any reason.

Universal default happens when a lender enforces default terms (usually imposed on borrowers who have missed payments or exceed balances) on a borrower who has defaulted with another lender. The credit-card default rate is the highest interest rate charged by a creditor or lender, usually as a penalty for missing a payment, exceeding the credit limit, or having your credit-card payment returned for insufficient funds.

If you've got a universal-default clause on one of your credit cards, you may have to pay the default rate even if you always pay on that card as agreed. You don't have to actually default on the loan in question to suffer from universal default. Instead, you might trigger the clause by the things you do with other accounts.

New credit legislation went into effect in February 2010 that prevents credit-card issuers from implementing universal default by limiting their ability to raise interest rates on preexisting balances. Card issuers are still allowed to use universal default on future credit-card balances, but they must give at least forty-five days' advance notice of the change.

Minimum Payment: A Bad Habit

Good habits of credit-card usage include paying the balance in full each month. Pay only the minimum monthly payment, and you'll feel the aftereffects for a long time. It's like taking two steps forward and one step back. Your payment reduces the credit-card balance, but it also increases the amount of interest that has accumulated since your last payment.

Be aware that your credit-card company may charge you different interest rates for different transactions—such as new purchases, cash advances, and transferred balances from another credit card. Thanks to the Credit CARD Act of 2009, there's another great reason to pay more than the minimum. The amount of the minimum payment gets applied to the balance with the lowest APR, and any amount paid above that gets applied to the balance with the highest interest rate, such as cash-advance balances. This means that if you pay only the minimum month after month, balances with the highest interest rates will get paid off very slowly, or possibly not at all.

Know Your Money

Minimum monthly payments are convenient, but they're a financial trap. Don't fall into it. A good habit is to pay your balance in full so you can use someone else's money for a little bit and avoid interest charges. If you can't pay in full, you are probably starting to charge too much. Use cash for a while.

Exercise

Credit-Card Minimum Payments

Let's take a look at a credit card that has a balance of $1,000, calculates the minimum payment by 2.5 percent of the balance due, and has an APR of 18 percent. When you break the APR down into twelve monthly periods (18 ÷ 12 = 1.5) you end up with a 1.5 percent finance charge per month.

For the first month, your minimum payment is $25 ($1,000 × 2.5 percent), which includes $15 ($1,000 × 1.5 percent) for that month's finance charge ($1,000 × 1.5 percent), leaving only $10 ($25 − $15) to be applied to the outstanding balance, reducing your debt.

For month two, your remaining balance is $990 ($1,000 − $10) so your next minimum payment would be $24.75 ($990 × 2.5 percent), which includes $14.85 ($990 × 1.5 percent) for that month's finance charge, leaving only $9.90 to be applied to the outstanding balance.

As you can see, this is a financial trap. After two months, you have made almost $50 in payments ($25 + $24.75) yet only reduced your original debt by $19.90 ($10 + $9.90). If you were to continue paying only the minimum and the features of this card remained unchanged, it would take 156 months or almost thirteen years to pay off that $1,000 initial balance.

This would result in paying $1,594.28 in interest alone. That's right—the interest is more than the original balance!

Application Denied: Next Steps

If you apply for a card in your name and you're denied, you have a few options.

Piggybacking

With piggybacking, you essentially borrow someone else's good credit history, usually your parents'. Here's how it works: Cardholders with good credit allow someone with no credit—such as yourself—or someone with bad credit to be an authorized user on their credit cards, or a joint account holder. The positive history of that account is reflected in the new user's credit report, regardless of whether he or she ever uses the account. This score boost makes it easier for the new user to get his or her own credit in the future.

It's important to remember that with piggybacking, your credit mistakes will become your parents' credit mistakes, just as their mistakes will become yours. If you're not confident that your parents use credit responsibly, it won't do you any good to share a credit history with them.

Get a Cosigner

Perhaps a parent or someone else with good credit would be willing to cosign your application for a credit card. If you pay on time, you'll build a good credit history. But if you don't pay on time or completely ignore your bills, the cosigner will be held legally responsible for your charges—and negative marks will end up on both of your credit reports. Never cosign for another young adult's credit application; you have too much to lose and nothing to gain. It's okay to get help from your parents when needed, though—they're invested in your success!

Student Offers

College students get plenty of credit-card offers, even if the student doesn't have any income. The flood has slowed in today's credit crunch but hasn't stopped, and lenders are betting that parents are supplying kids with cash while they're in school. If you're still in school, you can probably find offers at your dorm, student center, or elsewhere on campus. Be careful and only apply for one card.

Secured Cards

These credit cards pose no risk to the lender. As the borrower, you deposit money in an account held by the lender and get a credit card with a spending limit equal to your deposit. The lender knows if you don't pay, it can access the bank account to be repaid. If you go this route, make sure you apply for a card that reports activity to the credit bureaus so you can establish a positive credit history. To learn more about secured cards, check out the credit-cards section of websites like CreditCards.com.

Exercise

Credit-Card Terms

Before you get your first credit card—and certainly before you go putting purchases on plastic—become familiar with common credit-card terms. By taking a few minutes to educate yourself about how your credit cards work, you can prevent mistakes before they happen, and perhaps save yourself a lot of money and headaches down the road. Look up the definitions of important terms.

See appendix 1, "Exercises" for the list of terms.

Discussion

1. New cardholders often do not keep track of purchases and pay only the minimum payment each month. Why is this a bad habit?
2. What should you do instead?

Conclusion

Your credit-card usage is linked to your credit rating, which has a tremendous impact on your financial life both now and in the future. Whatever kind of card you start out with, you have it in your power to put yourself in an enviable position: a solid, clean credit history with a good credit score. Build it wisely and reap the benefits, or make mistakes and you'll pay a penalty for many years to come. Don't charge more than you can pay, and try to pay in full so you don't face interest charges. Make sure to pay on time, even if you can't pay in full. Making a minimum payment is a bad habit. Stay away from credit cards with a universal clause.

See appendix 2, "Reference Material," for more credit-card information.

8

CREDIT SCORE AND REPAIR

A credit score in the United States is a number representing the creditworthiness of a person. Credit scoring tries to predict your behavior—will you or will you not repay the loaned money as expected, according to preset terms and conditions? If you have no credit history, or any negative or derogatory remarks in your credit history, then it's easy for lenders to reject your application to borrow money.

Credit: Good And Bad

Good credit is based on your credit and payment history gathered over a period of time. This includes payments on credit cards and department-store cards; rent and mortgage payments; car payments; insurance payments; or payments made to anyone on a time payment. All of your payment history is collected each month by each of these individual companies and reported to all or one of the credit bureaus. When you have good credit, you have the means to secure the financing you need for anything, and that just makes life easier. The better your credit, the lower the interest rates you can secure on mortgages, car loans, and credit cards.

Bad credit indicates that, for whatever reason, you haven't been able to keep up with your financial responsibilities. Now, it's important to realize that not everyone who has bad credit is an irresponsible person. Lenders and others may seem to want you to feel that way, but in reality, they have no idea about your credit other than what they see on paper.

Regarding your credit score, it is important to know that how much debt you have is just as relevant as how you repay it. When you owe a small amount of money that you consistently repay, this tells lenders that you're not afraid of having a little bit of debt for which you are responsible, and this raises your score. If you have all your debt paid off, you are telling lenders that you don't really want any debt unless you are forced to have it, and that lowers your score. If you've used most of your credit, you will also lower your score even if you make consistent payments.

What Is FICO?

The early pioneer in credit scoring was Fair, Isaac and Company (founders Bill Fair and Earl Isaac, 1956), which eventually went public in 1987 with the NYSE stock symbol FICO. Today, the FICO scoring services are used around the globe by lenders, such as banks and credit-card companies, to evaluate the potential risk posed by lending money to consumers.

FICO scores, according to www.myfico.com, range from 300 (poor) to 850 (excellent). The average US score has remained steady since 2006 at between 680 and 720. The average for the eighteen to twenty-four age group is 638, but you can easily achieve 700 by the time you are twenty if you do things right.

There are three US companies—Equifax, TransUnion, and Experian—that collect credit-based information about you. These are referred to as *credit bureaus* or *credit reporting agencies*. It's important to understand that this is a process, and as with any process, the information collected will not always be accurate and changes all the time.

Credit Scores

You can obtain your FICO credit score—the ones lenders use—from MyFico.com. You'll probably have three different scores from the three different bureaus, largely because the bureaus don't all share the same data. One bureau may list more accounts for you than another, for example, and the differences (in types of accounts, payment histories, credit limits, and balances) will be reflected in the score that the bureau computes for you. The following chart shows a range of possible scores:

Score	Rating
350–450	Very poor—you are not creditworthy
450–500	Poor—low credit status or you currently have no credit
500–600	Average risk—can get credit but with higher interest
600–700	Acceptable credit—average interest rates, but problems exist
700–750	Very good credit—no problems acquiring credit
750–850	Excellent credit—superior score, lowest interest rates

---

Know Your Money

Because of differences in reporting to the credit bureaus, you should examine your credit reports from all three bureaus before you apply for a big loan, such as a car loan or mortgage. Many lenders take the middle score from the three bureaus when making their decisions, so fixing errors in all three reports before you shop for a loan is smart.

What Is Not in Your Score

FICO does not consider your race, color, religion, national origin, sex, marital status, or age. Additionally, it does not consider where you live, your occupation or employment history, your salary, any interest rate being charged on a particular account, or whether or not you are participating in a credit-counseling program.

What Is in Your Score and How It Is Calculated

A FICO score takes into consideration many factors, not just one or two. Your score includes positive and negative information in the following five categories. In general, late payments and too much debt will lower your score, while a good track record of on-time payments and steady long-term credit relationships will raise it.

1. *Payment history (35 percent)*: This category includes information about the way you paid your credit accounts in the past, including late payments and bankruptcies. FICO gives you points for maintaining good payment relationships. It considers whether you make your payments on time (paid as agreed) or not (past due), the number of past-due items on file, the number of accounts in collection, and how frequent and recent any problems have been. The impact of an item on your score depends on what other information is in the report. For instance, one late payment may not affect your score significantly if the rest of your history is good. The model looks at credit patterns, not isolated mistakes.

2. *Amounts owed (30 percent)*: The amount of credit you are using and the amount of credit still available are of interest to those setting your credit score. FICO considers the number of balances recently reported, the average balance across all trade lines, and the relationship between the total balance and total credit limit for both credit lines and installment accounts. FICO considers your current level of borrowing and whether you are close to or over your limit. Carrying too much credit is held against you even if you do not have balances on those cards.

3. *Length of credit history (15 percent)*: The number of months your credit accounts have been on your credit

report is a factor in your credit score. Every time you apply for credit or a loan, the bank or department store makes inquiries as to your credit score. FICO looks at how long you have had your account, the time since the account was last used, new accounts opened, the number of recent inquiries, and the amount of time since the most recent inquiry. The scoring model considers inquiries because statistics show that those anticipating financial troubles try to increase the number of credit lines they have available. The FICO model has taken into account certain lender practices that normally would negatively affect your credit report.

4. *Types of credit used (10 percent)*: FICO looks at the diversity of credit you use, including bank cards, travel and entertainment cards, department-store cards, personal finance-company references, and installment loans. FICO only looks at information in your credit report, and not all credit is reported.

5. *Pursuit of new credit (10 percent)*: The number of recently opened accounts, the number of times you've applied for credit in the recent past, reestablishment of positive credit history following past payment problems, and diversification of credit types are all noted.

Transactions That Hurt Your Score

- *Late payments:* A late or missed payment will hurt a good score more than a bad one, dropping a 700-plus score by 100 points or more.
- *Using nearly all of your available credit (credit limit)*: The gap between your balances and your available credit is important. Transferring balances from high-limit cards to lower-limit cards impacts the gap.
- *Consolidating credit accounts:* In general, it's better to have smaller balances on a few cards than a big balance on one card.

- *Shopping for a loan for a long time:* If you want to minimize the damage from credit inquiries, make sure that when you shop for a loan you do so in a fairly short period of time. The FICO score treats multiple inquiries in a fourteen-day period as just one inquiry and ignores all inquiries made less than thirty days prior to the day the score is computed.

Credit Repair

Forget the blame game. If you have poor or mediocre credit scores, you need to do some work to repair them. The reporting agencies can tell you what the reported problems are (see appendix 2, "Reference Material."). Focus on fixing those items rather than problems that were not reported. Once you've hit the 700 mark, improvements tend to have less of a positive impact. If your scores are in the "excellent" category, 750 or above, you'll probably be able to eke out only a few extra points despite your best efforts. There's really no point, anyway, since you're already qualified for the best rates and terms.

Know Your Money

You improve your credit score by paying your bills on time, paying down your debt, applying for credit sparingly, and correcting errors. A poor score will not haunt you forever, because a score represents a point in time.

Tips for Improving Your Credit Score

- *Pay down your credit cards.* Credit-scoring formulas reward a nice big gap between the amount of credit you're using and your available credit limits. Getting your balances below 30 percent of the credit limit on each card can really help. A good strategy is to pay off the highest-rate card that is closest to its limit first, then the second highest-rate card closest to the limit, then the third, and so on.

- *Use your cards evenly.* Racking up big balances can hurt your score, regardless of whether you pay your bill in full each month.
- *Check your limits.* Your score might be artificially depressed if your lender is showing a lower limit than you've actually got. If you consistently charge the same amount each month, it may look to the credit-scoring formula like you're regularly maxing out that card.
- *Dust off an old card.* The older your credit history, the better. The score tracks the length of your credit history, so shutting older accounts can make your credit history look younger than it actually is. It can hurt your score when issuers stop updating those accounts at the credit bureaus. Use your oldest cards every few months to charge a small amount, paying the balance off in full when the statement arrives.
- *Request some goodwill.* If you've been a good customer, a lender might agree to simply erase that one late payment from your credit history. You usually have to make the request in writing, and your chances of a "goodwill adjustment" improve the better your record is with the company. A longer-term solution for troubled accounts is to ask that they be "re-aged." If the account is still open, the lender might erase previous delinquencies if you make a series of twelve on-time payments.
- *Apply for new credit sparingly.* Applying for and getting an installment loan can help your score if you don't have any installment accounts.
- *Change significant errors.* Your credit score is calculated based on the information in your credit report, so errors there can really cost you. Indications of identity theft—anything that suggests your file has been mixed with someone else's delinquencies or accounts that aren't yours—should be reported immediately. Other items that

71

are usually worth the effort to correct with the bureaus include the following:

O late payments, charge-offs, collections, or other negative items that aren't yours
O credit limits reported as lower than they actually are
O accounts listed as anything other than "current" or "paid as agreed" if you paid on time and in full
O negative items older than seven years that should have automatically fallen off of your report

Here's the stuff you typically should not worry about:

O various misspellings of your name
O outdated or incorrect address information
O old employer listed as current

Some consumers also have had luck disputing old items with a lender that has merged with another company, which can leave lender records a real mess.

Discussion

1. Why should you care about your credit rating?
2. Why does your score change?
3. Is the pursuit of the highest credit score possible (720+) worth the effort? Remember, with good credit you have the means to secure the financing you need for anything, and that just makes life easier.

Conclusion

Maintain a good credit history to qualify for credit when you most need it—faster and at better interest rates. You can improve your credit score by paying your bills on time, paying down your debt, applying for credit sparingly, and correcting errors. A poor score will not haunt you forever because the score represents a point in time. As the information changes, so does your score; that is why lenders want the most current report to make the best decision. Fixing errors in all three reports before you shop for a loan is a smart move.

9

DEBIT VERSUS CREDIT CARDS

Putting something on "plastic" no longer necessarily means using a credit card. Today, debit cards are common—but do you know the difference and which one is better for you? Only you can decide if traditional credit cards or newer debit cards meet your needs, so understand the differences between them. Whichever you choose, be sure to know how much is in your bank account and write down and keep track of your purchases so you can compare them to your monthly bank statement or credit-card bill.

Debit-Card Usage: "Pay Now"

Debit cards were originally ATM cards, but now they have more uses. So what's the difference when the merchant asks for your debit or credit? No matter which option you choose, the money comes from the same place—your checking account or savings account. The money just comes a little faster when you're using a debit card, and there's no credit involved.

When you say "debit," you provide your PIN (personal identification number) to complete the transaction. The money for your purchase is taken immediately and directly from your bank account. Some debit cards look like credit cards and have a

Visa or MasterCard logo; you may even sign a receipt like a credit card. But unlike a credit card, the money is taken immediately and directly from your bank account. You'll want to make sure the money is there to be taken.

Most merchants would prefer you to use a debit card, as they avoid the credit-card fee and still get their money fast. Advantages of a debit card include the following:

- *Debit cards have no interest and are easy to use.* It's more convenient to carry a card than cash or a checkbook, and because you do give the money right away, you avoid the interest associated with buying on credit.
- *It's debt you can afford.* If the money isn't in your account, the transaction won't be completed.
- *You have a PIN number.* You select the PIN so it is easy to remember.

Know Your Money

Protect yourself from financial fraud, DO NOT give your PIN to others.

There are also disadvantages to debit cards:

- *There's a much greater liability risk.* Your entire bank account can be removed if your debit card is used fraudulently, which doesn't happen with credit cards. It's harder to get your money back, as your bank takes time to investigate, and there's no certainty they'll refund your money. In the meantime, you could bounce checks to your landlord or other companies. If your card is lost or stolen, be sure to report it immediately to your bank to prevent unauthorized access to your account. There are laws to protect you and limit your liability, but you must inform the bank (within twenty-four hours is best).

- *There's no grace period.* The money is removed from your account very quickly.

Credit-Card Usage: "Pay Later"

When you use your credit card, you provide your signature to complete the transaction. The money is taken from the credit-card company, which makes you a loan that you repay at a later date according to the loan terms (including line of credit, maximum spending limits, and cost of borrowing). Merchants pay a fee (usually 2 to 3 percent) to the credit-card company every time they accept the buyer's card for payment of a purchase in exchange for getting their money fast from the credit-card company. Advantages of credit cards include the following:

- *You have financial flexibility.* Even if you don't have the money right now, you can still make a large purchase, get emergency funds, or consolidate debt from other lenders. You can pay the money back in a way that fits your budget over a longer period of time.
- *You earn rewards.* Many credit-card companies offer rewards for using the card, such as money back on select purchases.
- *Credit cards are secure.* They're excellent for shopping online because they protect you by limiting your fraud liability to about fifty dollars.
- *You build a credit history.* Good use and timely payments help build a higher credit score, which helps you save money on large purchases like a car or house.

There are also disadvantages to credit cards:

- *It's debt you can't afford.* Credit cards are easy to use, even when you don't have the money to repay the loan. Even though you may have a high line of credit (such as $20,000 maximum), be aware of what you can afford in monthly payments and do not exceed that borrowing limit. If spending is getting out of control, leave your credit cards home.

- *You pay interest and fees*. Borrowing using credit cards can be expensive, with interest rates from 10 to 29 percent. So pay your bill in full, or else your real cost of purchasing things becomes a lot higher.

Match the Card to the Situation

Although both debit and credit cards have advantages, some situations are better suited for using a credit card rather than a debit card. These include the following:

- *Online purchases*—Debit cards are linked to your personal bank accounts, making you vulnerable to fraud if the card gets hijacked. Credit cards limit your liability.
- *Big-ticket items*—You have better dispute rights with a credit card if something goes wrong with the merchandise, and some cards offer extended warranties or insurance.
- *Deposits*—Use a credit card to leave a deposit (such as when renting equipment), and no money will be taken from your bank account unless you fail to return the equipment.
- *Restaurants*—You usually lose sight of the card when you use it to pay the bill, making restaurants one of the most common places for theft. Credit cards offer more protection in that situation.
- *Buy now and take delivery later*—Again, you have better dispute rights if something goes wrong with the merchandise.
- *Recurring payments*—With a debit card, a payment you forgot about (or shouldn't be charged, like a canceled gym membership) can be pulled out of your account, leaving you short of funds. With a credit card, you have time to dispute the charge before paying it.

- *Future travel*—If you're not traveling for another two months, don't give up your money so soon. Also, don't let your debit card info hang around until you arrive.
- *Hotels*—They block your card for $100 or more in case you run up a minibar bill or trash the room.

Discussion

Many merchants, like gas stations and hotels, don't know how much money you will spend with them, but they want to make sure you can afford it. So they will "block" your card, which means they'll authorize and reserve money in your account before your final transaction occurs. Gas stations can block $50 to $100 before you pump the gas. If you only buy $25 worth of gas, the remaining amount won't be released for up to three days. What does this mean for you?

Conclusion

Debit cards are convenient, with few fees, but they don't contribute to your credit history and leave your bank accounts more vulnerable to fraud. Credit cards only offer a credit option—a loan you must repay—but have better fraud liability protection. In general, debit cards are best for small payments you can easily pay in full, and for which you can avoid problems by comparing receipts to your bank statements each month. For most people, having both a credit and a debit card makes sense. Either way, do not spend more than what you have to pay, and you'll enjoy the benefits that each card provides.

10

PROTECT YOUR FINANCIAL INFORMATION

Today, we must share financial information frequently to get things done, whether through online purchases, payroll direct deposit, check writing, or loan applications. It is smart to be cautious when handing out your information to limit other people's access. Be sure to protect your information in both paper-based and online transactions. In this chapter, we'll discuss identity theft, lost wallets, and good record-keeping systems.

Know Your Money

There are new and affordable services that can help you prevent identity theft, such as LifeLock (http://www.lifelock.com). Enroll in one before you lose your wallet with all your credit cards.

Identity Theft

This crime occurs when con artists steal personal information (such as credit-card numbers and social-security numbers) to take advantage of your good credit history. They then set up new credit-card accounts, charge purchases to existing accounts, or drain bank accounts. Consumers often do not know that their credit identity has been stolen until they get bills for a credit card they never opened or charges they did not incur. Keep a record of all your credit-card account numbers and expiration dates in a safe place, along with the phone number and address of each credit-card company.

The following are some simple commonsense things you can do to protect yourself against identity theft:

- With the increased popularity of online systems, make sure you use complex passwords, secure websites (look for a padlock icon in the browser and https rather than http), and automatic timeouts from websites you've logged into but stopped interacting with.
- Don't sign blank checks or allow another person to fill in the amount.
- Enroll in an identity-protection program. You'll get alerts to help you avoid financial transactions related to identity theft before they become a problem.
- Don't leave a paper trail or your valuable things in plain view. Always take your ATM, gas station, and credit-card receipts with you. Save receipts to compare them with your billing statements.
- Shred bills, receipts, preapproved credit-card offers, and forms that contain personal information before tossing them in the trash.
- Be defensive with your personal information. Ask companies that require this information about their privacy policy and have them ensure that the information will not be shared with anyone else.

- Carry fewer credit cards, but when you do carry them, do so separately from your wallet or purse. Watch your card during a transaction and ask that it be returned quickly.
- Do not sign the back of your credit cards; instead, write "photo ID required."
- When paying your credit-card bill with a check, do not write the full credit-card account number on the check. Instead, put the last four digits (xxxx xxxx 4166). The credit-card company already knows the rest of the number, and anyone handling your check will not have access to it.
- Don't let websites "store" your cards or your passwords.
- Never give out personal or account information over the phone or Internet unless you've initiated the contact. Call the customer-service line yourself to confirm that a call or e-mail is legitimate.
- Give out your social-security number only when necessary. Substitute another number on a driver's license or an ID card when possible. Never have your social-security number printed on your checks. You can write it on if necessary.
- When traveling, carry a photocopy of your passport whenever possible instead of the original.
- Use a locked mailbox or install a slot in your door for mail delivery.
- Review each of your three credit reports each year to make sure the information is accurate.

Lost Wallet

When you lose your wallet, act fast—your personal identification is a gold mine for thieves. Call family or friends, and retrace your steps if possible to ensure that it really has been lost. If it's not found quickly, you should contact key organizations to prevent financial loss through fraud.

Credit-Card Companies

Explain you have lost your card, and give the time, place, and amount of money on the last transaction you know you made. Say that you want your account flagged for unusual spending patterns. These alerts can be placed without closing the account. Major credit-card companies can cancel your account number and send replacement plastic to you anywhere in the United States within twenty-four hours. You'll need to inform merchants with recurring charges of the new account. The Federal Trade Commission reminds you to select different PINs and passwords for the new accounts.

Division of Motor Vehicles and Police Department

Replacing your driver's license is more difficult than replacing credit cards and usually requires a visit to the DMV with all your backup documentation (passport, birth certificate, social-security card, etc.). The report can help police catch the thief via a traffic violation stop. Although not required, it's a good idea to file a police report as well, and keep a copy on hand. This will validate your story in case unusual purchase show up on your credit card.

Credit Bureau

Pick any one of the top three reporting agencies to tell about the loss, and it will inform the other two. A temporary alert will last about ninety days; a permanent alert remains for seven years. To remove the alert, you must make a request in writing along with proof of your identity. The contact information is as follows:

- *Equifax*: 800-525-6285, or PO Box 740241, Atlanta, GA, 30374-0241.
- *Experian*: 888-397-3742, or PO Box 9532, Allen, TX, 75013.
- *TransUnion*: 800-680-7289, or Fraud Victim Assistance Division, PO Box 6790, Fullerton, CA, 92834-6790

Your Local Bank

If you've lost personal checks or an ATM card, let your bank know so that your account can be closed, a new one can be opened, and unwarranted merchant and ATM transactions can be prevented.

Know Your Money

Before you lose your wallet, create a list of issuing bank customer-service numbers. Take a moment to put key items from your wallet onto a copy machine, and copy both sides of your license, credit cards, passport, and other items. Now you will know what you had in your wallet and all the account numbers and phone numbers to call and cancel. Keep the photocopies in a safe place.

Record-Keeping

Sometimes you need the right documentation to get things fixed or a reminder to get things paid on time. Where are those records when you need them? A system for personal records is a necessity. No matter how modest your home might be, you need a special place to keep your papers. This could be as elaborate as a room or home office or as simple as a corner of the kitchen or bedroom.

Regardless of the filing system used, records should be reviewed at least once a year so you can discard items no longer needed. January is a good time for an overhaul, since it's just before you begin to work on taxes. Good record keeping will help you:

- keep track of financial obligations (unpaid and paid),
- prepare tax returns,

- recover from a disaster (such as fire or burglary), and
- analyze your spending habits and tax obligations.

The better your record-keeping system, the better the available information, and the better decisions you'll make. You should keep two home files in addition to your safe-deposit box at the bank. These two files are your active file and your dead storage file. After two years, move the active file items to your dead storage file for another five years.

Your active file will hold the following:

1. Unpaid bills until paid
2. Paid bill receipts
3. Current bank statements
4. Current cancelled checks
5. Income-tax working papers

Keep your records up to date and secure to help you avoid penalties for late payments and minimize the risk of identity theft. See appendix 2, "Reference Material," for a good list of key documents to keep in a safe place.

Tax Records

How long should you keep tax records? The Internal Revenue Service has three years in which to audit federal income-tax returns. However, this limit does not apply in unusual cases. If you failed to report more than 25 percent of your gross income, the government has six years to collect the tax or start legal proceedings. Also, there are no time limits if you filed a fraudulent return or if you failed to file a return. The IRS generally keeps records for six years.

You don't have to keep everything for tax purposes, though. You can lighten your record load by discarding certain checks and bills once they have served their purpose. For example, you can throw away weekly or monthly salary statements—assuming you are paid in that way—after you check them against your annual W-2 form. But save cancelled checks that relate directly to an entry on your tax return, and keep all medical bills for three years to back up your cancelled checks.

Household Inventory Records

If there is a fire or burglary in your home, this record will help you remember what has to be replaced and how much each item is worth. An inventory also may show that you need to increase your insurance because your possessions are worth more than you thought. When you make your inventory, start at one point in the room and go all the way around, listing everything.

For each item, list what it is, how much it cost, when it was purchased, and what it would cost to replace it. Include the model number, brand name, dealer's name, and a general description. If you take pictures of the rooms and your household possessions, it will make identification or replacement easier. Arrange expensive collections, silver, and jewelry separately and take close-up pictures.

When you have finished all the rooms, including the basement, garage, and attic, add up the total replacement cost. That figure will represent what your household is worth and is what your insurance should cover. Update your inventory every six months or so by adding new purchases and adjusting replacement costs. Be sure to keep your inventory in a safe place away from your home (avoid losing it due to fire), such as a bank safe deposit box.

Safe-Deposit Box

If you don't have a safe-deposit box, consider getting one. The yearly rental at your bank or savings-and-loan company is inexpensive. Often the smallest size is adequate, though larger sizes are available at slightly higher charges. If you store documents from investment properties or securities, the rental can be claimed as a deduction for income-tax purposes. The box should not be used as a catch-all for souvenirs and unimportant papers.

Discussion

1. Describe how you can make it more difficult for con artists to gain access to your personal information. What things have you done for yourself already?
2. Do you already have a good record-keeping system?
3. Is any of your information available to the public (for example, on social media sites)?
4. It's hard to stay organized over the long term, so what are some good habits you can develop in that area?

Conclusion

Protect your personal information and report a problem quickly. Identity theft is growing and damages your credit rating for many years. Use common sense when issuing your personal information to others—don't sign anything you don't understand, let the bank protect your cash, be aware of scams, don't hand out your PIN, be cautious of joint accounts, and look for secure Internet websites before you conduct any online transactions. Put in place a good record-keeping system to keep you organized so that you'll have the information you need when you need it.

See appendix 2, "Reference Material," for more information.

Part Three

GROW YOUR MONEY: PLANNING, BORROWING, INVESTING, AND SAVING

A key to financial independence is learning to manage your money and not letting your money manage you. What if you spend more than you have? Is it okay to borrow? What should you be saving?

The following chapters guide you through the key information you need to plan where your money will come from and go to *before* you get it or spend it. Understand what to do with your money, and you will successfully navigate your transition to financial independence. All you have to do is know your money. So let's get started, first with personal planning and budgets, interest income (friend) and expenses (foe), and then investing and saving.

11

PERSONAL-PLANNING BASICS

Money problems arise when you spend more money than you have. To avoid this, begin by making a plan, one that is relevant to you—a personal plan.

A personal plan reflects who you are. It is a result of a process of defining your goals, developing steps to achieve them, putting the plan into action, monitoring progress, and modifying the steps as things change. Plans should be updated as a result of achieving goals, setting new priorities, and dealing with changing economic conditions.

Know Your Money

A key financial behavior for avoiding money trouble is living within your means. What does this mean? Simply put, keep your spending equal to or less than your income. Personal plans can help you avoid borrowing money from others—no debts, no frets. Don't try to live a bigger lifestyle than your income can provide.

Handling money is a key life-management skill. In order to know your money, you must understand where it comes from, where it goes, and how much you need to live on now and in the near future. Wasting money is easy, but it's not the objective. Traditional wisdom tells us that most people don't plan to fail, they simply fail to plan, and that if you don't know where you're going, any road will take you there.

Your money is limited, so you must distinguish your needs from your wants. Financially, you pay for your needs first and then your wants. Each person will define needs and wants differently; it's linked to your personality and how you think and feel about things. Wants are emotional—you dream of things you don't have, and there's usually not enough money for most of them after the needs get paid first.

To create your own personal plan, focus on these planning basics:

- needs versus wants
- setting goals
- record keeping
- budgets
- investments

This section will look at the first two items. Record keeping was discussed in chapter 10, and budgets and investments are the topics of chapters to come.

Life is a journey; it's easier to get to where you want to go if you understand who you are and have a plan to guide you. Your plan will help you achieve a goal, pause and celebrate a little, and then continue on to your future goals, no matter how big or small. Goals can be financial or nonfinancial, and they can help you prioritize which things to achieve first—and feel good about yourself once you achieve something.

Needs versus Wants

For most people, money is limited, so they must identify needs and wants. Financially, your needs must be taken care of first and then your wants. Needs like food, clothing, and shelter are essential for living. Wants increase the quality of living but are not essential—things like gourmet food, extra shoes, a big home.

What are your basic needs? First, assess your individual values—your beliefs and practices that are important enough for you to live in accordance with them. Examples include a strong work ethic, telling the truth, giving to charity, or being punctual. Did you think of being responsible with money? Identify some of your current life values:

1.

2.

3.

4.

Now identify your basic needs. These are things that are essential for living in the short term (one year or less).

1.

2.

3.

4.

Finally, identify your wants. These are things that increase the quality of living but are not essential. They must be prioritized, because it is easy to let desires for consumption and luxury outweigh our limited resources. So when you can afford one, what will come first?

1.

2.

3.

4.

Setting Goals

Without goals, maintaining a regular financial plan is a lot like maintaining a regular exercise program—easy to start, difficult to sustain. Goals help you avoid money problems that arise when you spend more than you have. Goals are destinations, something you want that you acquire through planned action. They can be near-term (see a movie) or long-term (debt free by age thirty), but goals should be meaningful to you and in line with your personal values. Your friends' goals may be cool, but they are not based on your values, so they won't mean as much to you. Goals are best set as minivictories to keep you motivated. Be sure you know when you achieve one!

Goals can be either financial or nonfinancial, and their purpose is to help you prioritize which things you'll achieve first. They should be personal—that is, meaningful to you so you can have a satisfying life. When you do achieve a goal, pause and celebrate a little, and then reset your future goals. You'll feel good about yourself as you avoid money problems and enjoy your journey through life.

To develop a goal, think of something big (save $1 million by age seventy) and then break it into smaller stepping-stones (save $250,000 by age fifty, $500,000 by age sixty) that are easier to attain. Goals cover different time horizons, with bigger goals taking longer to achieve. In general, a short-term goal is zero to three months, a medium-term goal is four to twelve months, and a long-term goal is greater than one year.

Goals should be SMART:

S	Specific	Buy an outfit to wear to work in the winter.
M	Measurable	Each month I will set aside $50.
A	Attainable	I can afford something worth $200 but not $500.
R	Realistic	Visit every baseball stadium on the East Coast.
T	Time-bound	Have enough money saved in four months.

Goal Mistakes to Avoid

Goals help define your future; they give direction to your plan of action. Stay motivated to achieve your goals. And when you're not motivated, ask yourself the following questions:

- Are my goals so vague I'm not sure how to get there?
- Do I know where the finish line is for each goal?
- Be honest—is the goal realistic or a fantasy?
- Am I sabotaging myself?
- Is procrastination my problem?

Examples of personal goals include the following:
Bad: I want to be rich and famous.
Better: I want to own a house in Florida.
Short: Save $30 in six weeks so I can go to the movies with my friends.
Medium: Purchase business attire (three outfits) before year-end.
Long: Save $1,500 per year for four years as a car down payment

You might want to create a chart to make sure your goals fit the SMART criteria:

Specific	Measurable	Attainable	Realistic	Time-Bound
Fit into skinny jeans	Zip up all the way	Yes	Yes	Next birthday
Car down payment	$2,000 each year	Yes	Yes. Need $6,000	Three years - Summer

---

Exercise

Setting Goals

My goal: To save money.
Now make your goal SMART!

Specific: What specifically will I achieve?	Save $1,000
Measurable: How will I measure it?	Save $125/week
Attainable: Is it achievable by me now?	Yes, I'll set up automatic transfers from my checking to savings accounts
Realistic: Do I know how to go about it?	Yes, I'll transfer money before I spend it
Time-bound: By what date will I achieve it?	Two months from now

What rewards will I give myself?

- Save $500, get a manicure ($20)
- Save $1,000, get a full-body massage ($70)

Revised SMART Goal: _____

This goal should be clear and easily monitored, with a timeline and a reward.

See appendix 1, "Exercises," for the answer.

Discussion

1. What goals have you set for yourself? Did you convert them to SMART goals?
2. How do you reward yourself for achieving a goal?
3. Achieving goals often requires patience and willingness to give up something you want now in return for something better at a later time. When was the last time you demonstrated delayed gratification?

Conclusion

Goals are an integral part of financial independence. If you don't have a goal, get one. Start now with goals that are meaningful to you and in line with your personal values. Stay simple, monitor your progress, and update your goals periodically. Don't waste your time or money on unnecessary things; aspire to live within your means by reducing liabilities and increasing assets to achieve your financial goals, both short-term and long-term. You'll have both small and large victories—don't forget to celebrate along the way.

12

BUDGET BASICS

Simply put, when you know your money, you worry less about it and spend more time enjoying life's journey. The best advice, no matter what stage of life you are in, is that financial success can be your reality when you live within your means. No debts, no frets.

A budget is the cornerstone of a solid financial foundation—it helps you get to know your money. The good news is it's easy to do. Whether you have a little money or a lot of money, you still need a budget. For many young people, there's a fear that once you have a budget you will have to cut back on all the fun spending. However, without sitting down and creating a budget, it is really hard to know what expenses need to be cut, if any.

A successful budget will include categories that reflect the way *you* actually spend money. A common mistake is to try to fit your spending into somebody else's categories. A good budget is a personal plan, so customize it to make it your own. A budget has two purposes: to be a tool to increase your awareness of how and where you spend your money, and a guideline to help you spend your money on things that are important to you

Having a budget will help you gain control of your money, pure and simple. Successful businesses keep track of their income and expenses, and so should you. Live with confidence rather than going through life trying to stay one step ahead of your bills.

Budget Overview

Let's look at the four major parts of a budget: income, expenses, the bottom line, and adjustments.

Income

The first step in making a budget is to determine how much money you have coming your way—that is, your income. This is quite easy and typically only requires you to look at your pay stub. Of course, if you're married, you'll include your spouse's income as well. In addition to your regular pay, add in any other sources of income you may have, such as interest, dividends, or a side business.

Expenses

Now that you know how much money you have coming in, look at the money that's going out—your expenses. Start with the everyday common things you regularly spend money on (such as rent, car payments, insurance, taxes). These are usually fixed expenses, meaning you can't easily change the amount that is due each month and they don't change as your income goes up or down.

After you've listed fixed monthly expenses, dig deeper to find out where the rest of your money goes. Take out your checkbook or recent bank statement for more information. Jot down how much you spend on things like utilities, groceries, entertainment, phone, Internet, and so on. Create a worksheet like the one used for the exercise later in this chapter to help you.

Joel Read

The Bottom Line

You should now have all the information needed to create your budget. Go ahead and total up your monthly income and all your monthly expenses. Subtract the expenses from the income, and you'll have your bottom line. If the number is positive, congratulations! You are spending less than you earn. If you have a negative number, be aware! You are spending more than you earn. Remember, the whole reason for creating a budget is to identify the financial gap and find out how to address it by changing your spending habits.

Adjustments

The goal of adjustments is to find ways to increase your income (more money coming in) and decrease your expenses (less money going out) so your bottom line will be zero or slightly positive. If you fail to make adjustments, then you will not gain control of your money, and soon your money will gain control of you.

Often you'll realize that by making just a few small adjustments to your spending habits, you can significantly improve your situation. Maybe this means eating out one time fewer a month or seeing the matinee show instead of the prime-time movie. Typically, saving a few dollars here and there can be enough to not only make sure you spend less than you earn but also allow you to either apply a few extra dollars to pay off your debt faster or start contributing to a retirement savings account.

Basic Budget Process and Details

Here is the basic budget process to get you started. Repeat this process as often as your life changes, or at least once a year.

1. Set up categories of spending.
2. Calculate your budgeted income, expenses, and bottom line.

98

3. Record your actual income, expenses, and bottom line.
4. Compare the actual results to the budgeted results (overall and by each category).
5. Set new goals and make budget adjustments to reflect new spending targets.

Let's look at these steps in a little more detail.

Set Up Categories

While basic categories like housing, utilities, and food apply to all of us, we each have expenses that are unique to our personal situation. For example, within the food category, if you regularly purchase lunch at work, you should create a subcategory for lunches. Think about your hobbies (crafts, video games, bicycling) and your habits (smoking, coffee, drinking) to help you identify other spending categories. The idea is to become more aware of your unique money behaviors—where your money goes—so you can make conscious and smart decisions about your spending.

Calculate Your Budgeted Amounts

To determine your monthly budgeted amounts for each category, it is important to walk a fine line between reflecting your actual expenses and setting targeted spending levels that will enable you to save money. Even seemingly fixed costs like housing or utilities can often be reduced.

Estimate your income by dividing your annual gross salary (before taxes and other deductions) and dividing by twelve for an average monthly income. Now do the same for other income such as interest, using your bank statements; dividends, using your stock statements; bonuses; and gifts, such as those received for birthdays or special events.

Estimate your expenses by looking ahead over the next six months and dividing by six for an average monthly expense.

Record Your Actual Income and Expenses

To get started, collect as many of your documents as you can—pay stubs, debit-card statements, checking-account statements, and a box of loose receipts. Don't forget to record your cash expenditures; jot down in a little notebook the cash you spend before you forget, and total it up at the end of the month. You will most likely be shocked at where your cash went. Finally, take all your expenditures and sort them into the spending categories you are interested in tracking.

Compare Actual Results to the Budget

Now sum up your actual income and expenses, being sure to include everything. If you used three months of data, divide by three to create a monthly average. Subtract the total expenses from the total income to arrive at your bottom line.

If you are fortunate enough to have a positive bottom line, be sure to transfer the excess amount into a savings or investment account at the end of each month. Extra cash left hanging around the house has a way of getting spent. If the bottom line is negative, focus on adjustments to get you headed in the right financial direction.

Set New Goals and Make Adjustments

Consider this a process of self-discovery. Many young adults don't have a clear idea of where their money goes until they start tracking their spending—and then they're usually surprised at how much they spend in certain categories over the course of a few months. Typically, just saving a few dollars here and there can be enough to make sure you spend less than you earn.

With your budgeting process mostly complete, you can take an in-depth look at your largest spending categories and brainstorm ways to reduce them, perhaps by adjusting your thermostat to reduce utilities or changing apartments to reduce housing costs. Don't overlook the smaller spending categories, as they are often the easiest to make adjustments to, and many small changes can add up quickly. Set a new spending goal for the next three to six months for each category.

If your actual bottom line was negative, your new adjusted budget should have a bottom line that is neutral—no savings, but no excess spending either. If your actual bottom line was positive, add a new expense category, such as savings/investment account, and contribute an amount that gives your new adjusted budget a bottom line that is neutral.

Repeat the process after another three to six months, compare your actual spending versus your revised budget, and learn more about yourself. Did you change your money behavior or not? Keep repeating this process every year or whenever something big changes in your life (new apartment, new job, marriage). Maintaining the budget process and heeding its message is a key skill for financial independence. You can do it!

Budget Guidelines: What Should You Be Spending?

Everyone has a different situation. Percentage budgeting is the best way to get started so you can establish a target percentage for each expense category. This process expresses your spending as a percentage of gross income; it shows you a way to measure your spending decisions and suggests areas in which to consider cutting back or spending a little more. These ranges clearly leave room for a lot for personal fine-tuning, and that flexibility is one of the advantages of the percentage method.

Here are the spending guidelines to help get you started.

Category	Income % (pretax)	Comment
Housing and utilities	20%–36%	Rent, utilities, insurance
Taxes	18%–30%	Federal, state, local
Health care	10%–13%	Medicine, doctors, hospital, insurance
Food	8%–12%	Groceries and dining out

Transportation	6%–15%	Medicine, doctors, hospital, insurance
Debt payments	6%–12%	All debt excluding car loan
Savings	5%–10%	Rainy-day fund, then retirement investments
Personal care	4%–8%	Clothes, hair, beauty products
Charity	1%–8%	If no money, volunteer!
Entertainment	1%–4%	Entertainment, travel
Other	TBD	Customize as needed

Again, you'll want to adjust this to your particular situation. For example, if you live with your parents, then you can move the budget money from housing to some other category. If you live in a major city, then your housing costs will be higher. Some people are perfectly happy subsisting on ramen noodles versus dining out, and others would rather save money than spend it on nice clothes.

Exercise

Create a Budget

Create your own individual budget. When complete, express each major spending category as a percentage of income (all categories should add up to 100 percent, no more or less). These percentages help you know how much of your income goes to housing or food.

Work with a friend so each of you creates your own budget. What makes you different from each other?

See appendix 1, "Exercises," for a chart to fill out.

Discussion

1. What did your first personal budget tell you? Is your bottom line positive, neutral, or negative? What does this say about your future financial behavior?
2. What are your current spending habits? Are you a saver or a spender? Do you spend compulsively or on planned purchases? What do you spend the most on, and what can you do to reduce this amount each month?
3. Do you have debt? If you have a negative bottom line, soon you'll have to borrow money, increasing your debt. Slowly, you'll begin to work for someone else—the lender. Is the lender interested in helping you improve your financial security?

Conclusion

A budget is the key tool to a solid financial foundation. It increases your awareness of how and where you spend your money, and it helps guide your spending toward the things that are most important to you. Compare your budget versus actual spending at least once a year so you can make adjustments and set new goals. Once you know where your money goes, you will make smart decisions and begin to save. If you fail to make adjustments, your money will likely control you. Always aspire to know your money, which means living within your means, and you will avoid many money problems throughout your life. You can do this!

13

INTEREST: FRIEND AND FOE

The biggest obstacle to having a higher net worth is the need to borrow money. Why? We all fight the constant desire to have more in our life and have it now. "Buy now and pay later" is a common theme, and with limited cash at hand we quickly turn to lenders. Advertisers make us think we need things whether we do or don't, and lenders make it easy to borrow. The downside is that borrowing money makes the things we buy more expensive. Until the debt is paid off, you are working for the lender, not for yourself.

Know Your Money

The basic principle of interest is the same whether you earn it (friend) or pay it (foe). So understand how interest works for you or against you. Of course, it's better to have it work for you. Don't forget, if you save first and buy with cash, then you don't have to borrow, and that makes purchases more affordable.

The Importance of Time

Thanks to the concept of compound interest, your original investment—called the *principal*—will grow over time because you are earning interest on your interest. The longer you leave that money alone, the more the accumulated interest grows, making your investment more valuable. Likewise, the longer you borrow money, the higher the interest you owe the lender, and the longer it will take you to get out of debt.

It takes time, but you can be a millionaire if you save a little bit over a long period. The two important factors in becoming a millionaire are:

- saving the most money you can each month, and
- getting the highest possible interest income on your investment.

As a young adult, you have nearly fifty years until you retire. You'll get to a million if you save $50 a month and earn a 10 percent interest rate, or save $250 a month and earn a 6 percent interest rate.

Interest Income

There are many investment options (see chapter 14, "Introduction to Investment Options"), but for now let's assume that you put your money in a bank savings account and the bank pays you interest on your money. Today's bank interest rates are a dismal 1 percent or less, but to help illustrate the concept of interest income, let's assume you deposited $4,000 on July 1, 2014, and the bank pays you 8 percent each year to use your money. How much money do you have in ten years?

Year	Date	Beginning Balance	Interest Income	End Balance
1	7/1/15	$4,000.00	$320.00	$4,320.00
2	7/1/16	$4,320.00	$345.60	$4,665.60
3	7/1/17	$4,665.60	$373.25	$5,038.85
4	7/1/18	$5,038.85	$403.11	$5,441.96
5	7/1/19	$5,441.96	$435.35	$5,877.31
6	7/1/20	$5,877.31	$470.19	$6,347.50
7	7/1/21	$6,347.50	$507.80	$6,855.30
8	7/1/22	$6,855.30	$548.42	$7,403.72
9	7/1/23	$7,403.72	$592.30	$7,996.02
10	7/1/24	$7,996.02	$639.68	$8,635.70

Note that 8 percent of $4,000 is $320 a year, times ten years = $3,200 (simple interest). However, you earned $4,635.70 ($8,635.70 – $4,000). Why? Each year, the bank pays you for the money you lent them *plus* the interest from previous years. This is called *compound interest*, and it is a very powerful tool to grow your savings. The longer you lend your money to the bank, the faster it grows, as the interest income gets bigger each year.

In this example, you earned compound interest of $4,635.70 versus $3,200 simple interest, so you received an additional $1,435.70. To earn the same $1435.70 at $10 an hour, you would have to work 143.4 hours, or about 3.6 weeks. So compound interest income is your friend, because it makes your money work for you instead of you working for your money.

The Power of Compound Interest

Keep $100 dollars in a box in your room for four years, and you still have $100. Give the $100 to a bank at 5 percent interest, and in four years you'll have $122. Each year, the bank pays you for the money you lent it plus the interest from previous years.

Compound interest works for you when you save (save more, faster) and against you when you borrow (owe more, faster). If you want to know how much interest you will earn on your investment or if you want to know how much you will pay above the cost of the principal amount on a loan or mortgage, you will need to understand how compound interest works.

Compound interest is paid on the original principal and on the accumulated past interest. When the interest is compounded once a year, the formula is

$$A = P\left(1 + r\right)^n$$

Where

- P is the principal (the initial amount you borrow or deposit)
- r is the annual rate of interest (percentage)
- n is the number of years the amount is deposited or borrowed for
- A is the amount of money accumulated after n years, including interest

Interest Expense

Interest expense is the opposite of interest income. As you know, debt is an obligation you must pay back with interest. Loans financially benefit the lender, not the borrower. It is so easy to get into debt but hard to get out of debt. A lender loans you money, and you must pay back the original amount borrowed—the principal—over a defined period of time. That time could be short, as in months, or long, as in years.

To help illustrate the concept of interest expense, let's assume you borrowed $4,000 at 8 percent interest for ten years starting on July 1, 2014. How much money do you owe the lender in ten years?

Year	Date	Beginning Balance	Interest Expense	End Balance
1	7/1/15	4,000.00	320.00	4,320.00
2	7/1/16	4,320.00	345.60	4,665.60
3	7/1/17	4,665.60	373.25	5,038.85
4	7/1/18	5,038.85	403.11	5,441.96
5	7/1/19	5,441.96	435.35	5,877.31
6	7/1/20	5,877.31	470.19	6,347.50
7	7/1/21	6,347.50	507.80	6,855.30
8	7/1/22	6,855.30	548.42	7,403.72
9	7/1/23	7,403.72	592.30	7,996.02
10	7/1/24	7,996.02	639.68	8,635.70

Note that 8 percent of $4,000 is $320 per year, times ten years = $3,200 (simple interest). However, you owed $4,635.70 ($8,635.70 – $4,000). Why? Each year you pay the lender for the money you borrowed *plus* the interest from previous years. This too is called compound interest, and it is very powerful tool to grow your debt. The longer you borrow the lender's money, the bigger the interest expense gets and the faster the debt grows.

In this example, you owed compound interest of $4,635.70 versus $3,200 simple interest, so you paid an additional $1,435.70. Whereas in the investment example compound interest was your friend, here it's your foe because it makes you work for your money instead of your money working for you.

Exercise

Simple versus Compound Interest

Simple interest is calculated by multiplying the investment amount by the interest rate and doing this again every year. Compound interest is calculated by multiplying the investment amount by the interest rate, and the next year the investment amount includes the interest. Each period includes the interest from the prior period. This means your investment grows faster. Let's see how this works by comparing $1,000 at 5 percent for five years. (Round decimals up.)

Simple	Year 1	Year 2	Year 3	Year 4	Year 5	TOTAL
Base Investment	$1,000	$1,000	$1,000	$1,000	$1,000	$1,000
Interest	$50					
Balance YE	$1,050					

Compound	Year 1	Year 2	Year 3	Year 4	Year 5	TOTAL
Base Investment	$1,000	$1,050	$1,103			
Interest	$50	$53				
Balance YE	$1,050	$1,103				

The same process works for borrowing or investing.

See appendix 1, "Exercises," for the answer.

Joel Read

Installment Loans

An installment loan is a way for a borrower to get money now and repay it over time through a set number of scheduled payments (regular installments). The most typical loan payment type gives each payment the same value over the life of the loan. The term of the loan may be as little as a few months, such as for a TV set, and as long as thirty years, such as for a home mortgage. The borrower will pay the interest on the loan each time period plus some fixed percentage of the amount borrowed. These payments will gradually reduce the amount borrowed—the principal—during the loan's life, a process called *loan amortization*. Because you are borrowing less each month, you pay less in interest. Since you have equal monthly payments, over time you gradually pay less in interest and more in principal until the principal is paid off.

Installment loans are generally considered to be a safe and affordable alternative to other loans or credit cards. Often a loan's payment obligations are enforced by a contract, which can place the borrower under additional restrictions known as *loan covenants*.

Exercise

Monthly Payments

You see an advertisement for flat-screen TVs on sale for $3,000. So on June 1, 2013, you purchase a new flat-screen TV system for $3,000, plus 7 percent sales tax ($210) and the cost of installation ($490), for a total of $3,700. The store offers you an installment loan with twelve monthly payments and an 18 percent interest rate. Here is your payment schedule:

No.	Payment Date	Beginning Balance	Payment (Principal + Interest)	Principal	Interest (Monthly)	End Balance
1	7/1/13	3,700.00	339.22	283.72	55.50	3,416.28
2	8/1/13	3,416.28	339.22	287.97	51.24	3,128.31
3	9/1/13	3,128.31	339.22	292.29	46.92	2,836.02
4	10/1/13	2,836.02	339.22	296.68	42.54	2,539.35
5	11/1/13	2,539.35	339.22	301.13	38.09	2,238.22
6	12/1/13	2,238.22	339.22	305.64	33.57	1,932.58
7	1/1/14	1,932.58	339.22	310.23	28.99	1,622.35
8	2/1/14	1,622.35	339.22	314.88	24.34	1,307.47
9	3/1/14	1,307.47	339.22	319.60	19.61	987.86
10	4/1/14	987.86	339.22	324.40	14.82	663.47
11	5/1/14	663.47	339.22	329.26	9.95	334.20
12	6/1/14	334.20	334.20	329.19	5.01	00.00
TOTAL			$4,076.64	$3,700.00	$376.64	

So what started out as a $3,000 TV ultimately cost $4,076.64 when you included sales tax, installation, and financing cost (+35.9 percent). Plus, for the next twelve months, you couldn't save any money, and your ability to borrow more for emergencies was limited.

Note that 18 percent of $3,700 is $55.50 each month. Multiplied by twelve months, it should equal $666. But as you pay down your debt and the original principal decreases, the interest expense also decreases. This saved you $289.36 ($666.00 – $376.64). Installment loans still cost you money, but they cost you less than simple interest each year on the purchase amount.

Debt-to-Income Ratio

It's a good exercise to figure out how much debt you have and compare that to how much you earn. This measurement helps you understand what debt load you can afford. Here's how to calculate your debt-to-income ratio:

1. Start with you debt load—what you owe. Include such things as student loans, credit cards, loans from friends and family, child support, and car loans. Add them up as both total amount due and monthly payment obligations.
2. Figure your gross annual earnings and divide that number by twelve for your monthly income.
3. Take your monthly debt-payment obligation and divide it by your monthly income. Slide the decimal two places to the right to make it a percentage.

Know Your Money

How much debt is too much? This varies from person to person, but general budget guidelines are to keep your debt at 20 percent or less of your gross income. Over 20 percent hurts your ability to borrow (meaning you would have to pay higher interest rates); 10 to 20 percent is manageable for good credit ratings; and 10 percent or less is outstanding. If you live in a high cost-of-living area, guidelines increase by 5 percent, but something else in your budget must be reduced.

Exercise

Car Payments

It's finally time to buy that car you always wanted. You've decided to save money by purchasing a used vehicle, not one on the top-ten stolen list. You have no trade-in vehicle but have negotiated

a great price with the dealer. The dealer offers
you an installment loan based on the following:

- car purchase price of $22,500
- sales tax of 7 percent
- title and tags at $325
- interest rate of 9 percent for above-average credit
  rating
- payment schedule of five years or sixty months

Calculate your payment schedule on a separate piece of
paper with this format:

No.	Payment Date	Beginning Balance	Payment	Principal	Interest (Monthly}	End Balance
1						
2						
3						
4 to 60						

What is the real cost of borrowing? If
you paid cash, what would you save?

See appendix 1, "Exercises," for the answer.

Discussion

1. Can you explain how the power of interest works against
   you or for you?
2. Your total debt should be what percentage of your
   budget?

Conclusion

Interest works the same way in investments (interest income) as it does in borrowing (interest expense). Borrowing money makes the things you buy more expensive. Loans benefit the lender, not the borrower. Installment loans are a relatively safe means of borrowing, but good money habits include saving for larger purchases and paying cash instead of borrowing. The biggest obstacle to higher net worth is when you borrow too much money.

14

INTRODUCTION TO INVESTMENT OPTIONS

Are you ready to invest? Have you paid down your debt and saved for an emergency? You're probably eager to get started and see your money work for you. But where do you start? What do you do? What are you going to do with the additional money and when do you need to use it? Are you hoping to take a trip next year, put down payment on a home in seven years, or build a retirement nest egg for thirty years down the road?

Each investment option you select should make you money. Some investments are safe but have a low rate of return, while others are risky but have higher returns (or higher losses). Your investment portfolio is the summation of all your individually separate investment actions. Yes, some types of investment are more straightforward than others, but no matter which you choose, you can take control of every one of them. Regardless of whether you make your own decisions or rely on the advice of others to guide you, you must know your money.

There are four key elements in determining how much money your investments will be worth: time, diversification, risk, and investment type. Let's look at each of those in more detail.

Time

Thanks to the concept of compound interest, your investment principal as well as the accumulated interest will continue to grow over time so that you are earning interest on your interest. The longer you leave that money alone, the more the investment and the accumulated interest will grow.

So ask yourself, how long are you investing for? Do you plan to invest for the next ten years? Twenty years? Thirty years? Do you anticipate needing to get to your money before your investment matures? The longer you leave the money in your investments alone, the more you will have in the long run. And remember—some investment types have penalties attached if you touch your money before the investment matures.

Also, how often do you plan to invest? Weekly? Monthly? Annually? The more consistent your investment schedule, the more your investment will grow. If you invest sporadically, you will probably not get as great a return.

Diversification

Diversification means you spread your money among different investments to reduce risk. By doing this, you can protect yourself from huge losses from a singular investment (type or industry). The more diversified your investments are, the less any one investment can hurt you if something blows up.

How should you diversify? Well, if you only choose to invest by buying stocks, you could be in big trouble if things go really bad with the stock market. A better strategy would be to spread your money out among different types of investments—stocks, bonds, and CDs—and industries.

You should know, though, that even if diversification reduces your risk, it doesn't eliminate it entirely. So before you decide to diversify your investments, talk to a financial expert. He or she will be able to guide you in the right direction.

Risk

A fundamental relationship exists between risk and reward: higher risks should deliver higher rewards. Higher risk also means there is a larger chance that you may not make any money, and in fact you may lose your investment entirely. The gain or loss on an investment over a specified period is called the *rate of return* or *return on investment* (ROI) and expressed as a percentage increase over the initial investment cost. Gains on investments are considered to be any income received from the security, such as a dividend, plus realized capital gains—the proceeds from selling the investment.

Each investment option has a different risk—a deviation from an expected outcome. The deviation can be positive or negative, and relates to the idea of "no pain, no gain." To achieve higher returns in the long run, you have to accept more short-term volatility. Future investment performance is not guaranteed, so if you want more than a 3 percent return—say, 10 percent—are you willing to accept the risk of losing 10 to 30 percent of your money in order to get the higher returns?

How Much Profit Did You Make with Your Investment?

To measure your total rate of return, use this formula:

$$\frac{(Value\ of\ investment\ at\ end\ of\ year\ -\ Value\ of\ investment\ at\ beginning\ of\ year) + Dividends}{Value\ of\ investment\ at\ beginning\ of\ year}$$

For example, if you buy a bank CD for one year with a minimum deposit of $1,000 and interest paid of $30, the rate of return is 3 percent:

$$\frac{(\$1,030 - \$1,000) + \$0}{\$1,000} = \frac{\$30}{\$1,000} = 0.03 = 3\%.$$

Note that for stocks, you need to include the dividends paid while you owned the stock.

Exercise

Rate of Return Calculation

You bought a piece of art for $1,500 and it has now been appraised at $1,950, so you have an unrealized gain of $450. It is unrealized because you haven't sold the painting yet. What is the total return?

$$\frac{\left(\$1,950 - \$1,500\right) + \$0 \text{ dividends}}{\$1,500} = \frac{\$450}{\$1,500} = 0.30 = 30\%$$

Two years later, you sell the art for $2,150. Now you have a realized gain—the money you received is real! What is the total return?

See appendix 1, "Exercises," for the answer.

Investment Type

There are many different ways to invest your money. Here, we'll discuss some of the most common opportunities you will find.

Certificate of Deposit (CD)

CDs are like savings accounts, but you have to deposit a specified minimum amount (usually at least $500) and leave it there for a specific period of time. The minimum, the rate of return, and the amount of time that you must leave your money in the account vary widely, from one month to ten years for the latter. CDs typically earn significantly more interest than regular savings accounts, and the longer you're willing to commit, the higher the interest rate you'll earn. Be warned, though, that if you withdraw money from a CD before it matures, you will probably have to pay a penalty.

Banks are the most common place to open a CD. You'll want to do some shopping around, because the minimum opening balance and interest rate will differ from bank to bank. When opening a CD, you'll have to provide the bank with basic information, such as your name, address, phone number, and social-security number, and you'll need to have your deposit money. Some banks will allow you to open a CD online.

Mutual Funds

Mutual funds are pools of money from different investors that are professionally managed and typically invested in a combination of things, like stocks and bonds. You can buy mutual funds from a bank or investment firm. They are usually a less risky way to invest than buying just one or two stocks on your own.

You can purchase mutual funds a few different ways. The least expensive is directly through the fund company itself. Contact the fund company to request information and a prospectus for the fund or funds you are interested in and ask what you need to do in order to make an investment in the fund. Banks, investment firms, brokerages, and insurance companies are also places from which you can typically purchase mutual funds. Keep in mind, though, that if you go through a third party to purchase mutual funds, there will likely be some fees involved. These fees reduce your rate of return.

Stocks

Refer to chapter 15, "Introduction to the Stock Market," for a description of various stocks and the stock market.

Bonds

When you purchase a bond, you are basically loaning money to a company or a government group (federal, state, or local), and you are paid interest for the use of that money over a specified period of time, generally a few months to thirty years.

If you hang on to a bond until it matures, the issuer guarantees that you will receive the original amount you paid plus interest. Bonds typically pay better interest than savings accounts or CDs, but you need to make sure you're loaning your money to a strong, secure company. There are several different kinds of bonds out there, including the following:

- *Government bonds*, which are issued by the federal government. The most common type of government bond is a savings bond or Treasury bond. These are typically pretty safe investments, but they also yield lower interest rates.
- *Municipal bonds* (also known as "munis") are sold by local governments, such as states and cities. They are often tax-exempt, which means you will pay no taxes on the interest you earn.
- *Corporate bonds* are issued by private and public corporations, usually in multiples of $1,000 and/or $5,000. The interest payments you receive from corporate bonds are taxable and, unlike stocks, do not give you an ownership interest in the company.
- *Convertible bonds* can be converted into shares of stock in the company that issues the bond, usually at a predetermined ratio.
- *High-yield bonds* (also known as *junk bonds*) are issued by organizations that don't qualify for investment-grade ratings by one of the leading credit-rating agencies, meaning the issuer is considered to have a greater risk of not paying interest in a timely manner. These bonds pay higher interest rates but are considered very risky.

There are a few different avenues you can take when you decide to purchase a bond. If you are interested in purchasing a government bond, such as a savings bond, check with your bank. You can also purchase government bonds directly from a government agency, such as the Federal Reserve. If you're interested in purchasing other types of bonds, such as corporate bonds, you can do so through an investment firm or a bond dealer.

Retirement Savings Accounts

401(k)

This investment option helps you save on your taxes *and* you get free money from your employer. Sounds like a no-brainer, right? You might be surprised by how many people choose not to participate in their company's 401(k) plan despite the obvious advantages. The IRS determines a maximum amount that can be contributed from your pretax salary, and those limits may change on a yearly basis.

A 401(k) is a retirement plan funded with your before-tax salary contributions and a matching contribution from your employer. The employee contributions, employer contributions, and growth in the 401(k) are all tax-deferred until withdrawn from the account. Here's how the tax-benefit portion of this savings plan works: The money you elect to contribute reduces your taxable income for that year, saving you money, and when you do withdraw money, you don't pay any taxes on it. If your employer has a matching program in which it contributes money into your 401(k) as part of your benefits package, you are not taxed on that money either.

Once money is deposited, you usually can't make any withdrawals before age fifty-nine, unless you have a special circumstance. If you do make an early withdrawal from your account, you will be hit with a penalty, generally 10 percent. In addition, you will lose the value of that money over time. So withdrawing money from the account significantly lowers the value of your investment.

As part of managing your 401(k) plan, you will typically be given several different investment options, including money-market funds, bonds, and stocks. You have the opportunity to decide how to divide your money among the available options.

The choices you make could have a huge impact on the value of your 401(k), so do some research before you invest.

Don't fail to invest in your retirement just because you don't plan to be in a particular job for long. Many employees today migrate from job to job pretty quickly—every few years or so. So start participating in your 401(k) as soon as you are eligible. When you leave a job, you can generally move your 401(k) into your new employer's plan or into a rollover IRA. Either way, you are still reaping all the benefits a 401(k) has to offer.

Individual Retirement Account (IRA)

An IRA is basically a savings account with lots of restrictions. The main advantage is that you defer paying taxes on the earnings and growth of your savings until you actually withdraw the money (when you're older and need it). The main disadvantage is that the tax law imposes stiff penalties if you withdraw the funds before you turn fifty-nine-and-a-half.

There are different types of IRAs, each with its own tax implications and eligibility requirements. For traditional, nondeductible, and Roth IRAs, the most you can contribute each year is $5,000. This was the maximum IRA contribution for the years 2008, 2009, 2010, 2011, and 2012. For the years 2013 and 2014, the maximum IRA contribution is $5,500.

A simple IRA is a group retirement plan, which allows an individual to deposit pretax dollars, so you don't pay any tax on this income until many years later when you withdraw the money. Add employer-matching contributions, and the benefits really add up.

You can deposit money into an IRA at any time during the year. And even after the year has ended, you can still deposit money before you file taxes (no later than April 15 without a filing extension). This may reduce your tax obligation.

Other

There are many other investment alternatives, including commodities, land, rental property, coins, precious metals, homes, cars, art, and rental equipment. Find something you're interested in following, and then follow the news for a while to learn about how things change.

Investment Risks

Each investment has its own unique set of risks that need to be understood prior to investing. In general, when you invest, you don't expect to lose your money but rather to make money at a particular rate of return. What is the chance that the actual return will be different from what you expected? This risk of a different outcome is driven by many factors, most of which are not under your control, so beware. They include market risk (a weak market reduces your investment), political risk (changes in law or political environment could reduce your investment), and company risk (the company performs poorly, reducing your investment).

You can reduce your risk by investing in strong, growing markets; safe countries with no political turmoil; well-managed companies with a good performance history; and many diverse companies in different industries. Learn all you can, and with smart decisions, you'll make your money work for you.

As an investor, you must decide what level of risk you are willing to accept in exchange for potential returns. This is referred to as the risk-return trade-off or iron stomach test. Usually low levels of uncertainty (low risk) are associated with low returns (low profit), and higher levels of uncertainty are associated with higher returns (profit).

If you cannot afford to lose your investment, then you need to focus on lower returns. If you can afford to lose some or all of your investment, then you may focus on higher returns.

Exercise

Employer Matching Programs

Here's how employer matching program and tax benefits work. Let's say you have a job making $40,000 a year, and you elect to put $5,000 into your IRA. You would not have to pay taxes on the $5,000 that you invested, and so would claim only $35,000 on that year's income-tax return. And if your employer has a matching program (such as 50 percent of your contribution) that deposits money into your IRA as part of your benefits package, you are not taxed on that money either.

Annual IRA Contributions (Savings)
- Employee contribution = $5,000
- Employer contribution = 50% of $5,000 = $2,500

Annual tax = 25 percent tax bracket

The benefits are that you save more money and reduce your tax bill. Calculate the total favorable impact for you. Is this a good investment or not?

See appendix 1, "Exercises," for the answer

Discussion

Try to rank the listed investment types for investment risk, from low to high. Each investment option has a different risk—a deviation from an expected outcome. That deviation can be positive or negative, and relates to the idea of "no pain, no gain."

To achieve higher returns in the long run, you have to accept more short-term volatility.

Conclusion

There are four key elements that determine how much money your investments will be worth: type of investment, risk, time, and diversification. Invest early and often, and the power of compounding interest will improve your rate of return. Diversify your investments to reduce the risk of catastrophic loss from a single investment. All investments vary in terms of risk, so it's okay to ask others to help you know your money so you can gain control.

15

INTRODUCTION TO THE STOCK MARKET

There are two markets that deal in company stocks. The first market, or primary market, is where a company issues stock directly to investors for the first time; this is called an *initial public offering* (IPO). After that, the company is publically owned—a corporation. There is a secondary market where shareholders go to sell their stock and get their money back from new investors. This secondary market is called the *stock market*.

One of the most famous stock markets is the New York Stock Exchange (NYSE). People often use the term *Wall Street*—the main street in New York City's financial district—to refer to the US stock market in general. From 1900 through 2012, the NYSE (the value of which is measured by an index called the *Dow Jones Industrial Average* or *DJIA*) has a historical rate of return of approximately 9.4 percent, comprised of 4.8 percent in stock-price appreciation and 4.6 percent in dividends paid. For 2013, the DJIA increased from 13,104 to 16,576 or +25.6 percent, a very good year.

Stock markets are like a shopping mall: lots of stores (company stocks for sale) and lots of shoppers looking for a bargain. Stock markets are also like an auction house: the stockbrokers act as auctioneers, matching buyers and sellers to create acceptable deals. The money exchanged comes from investors and not from the original company. No privately owned company stock can be bought or sold on the public stock exchange.

Over time, people usually earn more from owning stock than from leaving money in the bank, buying bonds, or making other investments. As the company earns money and grows, the profits are shared with the shareholders. Stocks are an investment option, so the four key elements to determine how much money your investments will be worth also apply to stocks as well as to other investments: investment type, risk, time, and diversification. See chapter 14, "Introduction to Investment Options," for more details.

New Values Every Day

Stock markets measure the current value of their member companies based on the capitalist economic principles of supply and demand. If supply exceeds demand, the price goes down and vice versa. So what makes the supply change? Every day there are sellers and buyers with certain expectations for the future, either near-term or long-term. Shareholders assess their expectations to be favorable (hold, buy) or unfavorable (sell). No one can accurately predict how the market will perform on any given day because there are just too many variables. News from any source can have an impact, and each piece of news can slow things down or speed things up. All buyers and sellers sort out the news and reset their expectations, which collectively are reflected in the current price of the stocks and the aggregate market value.

Here are some news categories that tend to influence the stock market:

- specific company performance and earnings
- war/terrorism
- crime/fraud
- interest rates/inflation

- energy/oil prices
- serious political unrest

Some of these have immediate impact and some have long-term impact. The market likes stable, quantifiable events with no surprises, so the factor with the most impact on the market is uncertainty. When surprises occur, raising the chance that things can change again, uncertainty increases, which in turn erodes the market's sense of control. Prices can jump up or down quickly and erratically.

In theory, stock markets are *efficient*, meaning stock prices change quickly because everyone has access to the same information at the same time. Although this may not be true, in a broad sense the market expects to know about all events, so with time the market value absorbs their impact. What this means to you is that these market bumps are just temporary and things will soon smooth out—no surprises. So pay attention to current events.

Stock-Market Sectors

Investors have developed ways to track stock performance. One is to put companies into similar categories, called *sectors*, for comparison purposes. The stock market is often broken into eleven sectors, of which two are *defensive* and nine are *cyclical*.

Defensive Sectors

Defensive sectors represent companies whose stock price does not suffer much from bad market news (market downturn) because people don't stop using their products. People never stop needing energy and food, so the two defensive sectors are utilities and consumer staples. Unfortunately, these stocks do not raise much from good market news because people don't use more of their products in a growing market.

Cyclical Sectors

Cyclical sectors represent companies whose stock price *does* change a lot as the market conditions change, sending prices rising and falling. Collectively, one sector can have prices rising while another sector is falling. The nine cyclical sectors are:

1. Basic materials
2. Capital goods
3. Communication
4. Consumer cyclical
5. Energy
6. Financial
7. Health care
8. Technology
9. Transportation

You can use sector information to compare how a stock you may want to buy is doing compared to other companies in the same sector. If other stocks are up 14 percent and your stock is up 3 percent, you need to find out why and decide whether to hold, buy, or sell. Likewise, if your stock is doing better than others, you'll want to find out why and decide whether to hold, buy, or sell.

Overall, there is a lot of information at your fingertips. Use the sector information to see how your stock is doing compared to its peers and decide if the stock you have is a potential winner or a potential loser. Then decide to hold, buy, or sell to balance your investment rate of return.

Stocks: Basic Features

Why do companies issue stock? If a company wants to grow, it needs money to hire people to build things to sell. It can get a loan from a bank, but that money would have to be repaid. By issuing stock, a company can raise money without having to repay it. Because it is not a loan, it is not debt, but is referred to as *equity*.

Before you become an equity investor, you need to review three important things:

1. Your personal financial goals and means
2. The state of the economy and stock market
3. Sectors with prospects for growth

Once you know how much you can invest and have a list of potential companies, you need to determine what kind of stock ownership you want.

Stock Ownership

Stock represents ownership in a company. Each unit is called a *share* and each owner of a unit of stock is called a *shareholder*. If a company issues one hundred shares and you bought three, then you would own 3 percent (3 ÷ 100) of the company. As the company earns money and grows, the profits are shared with the shareholders, which changes the stock price. Most shares also come with voting rights, so you have a voice in some company decisions. The more shares you have, the more voting power you have, and your voice (influence) in the company grows stronger.

Stock held by individuals is called *common stock*. These shares have some voting rights and allow the investor to share in dividends (although not all companies pay a dividend). When stock prices are quoted at being up or down, they are referred to as *common-stock prices*. When a company dissolves, it must pay all of its obligations, and only then will the common shareholders get paid from what's left over. Common shares are *liquid assets,* meaning it's easy to convert your stock to cash thanks to stock markets.

Preferred stock is similar to common stock in many ways, but the two important differences are no voting rights and preferential treatment regarding who gets paid first from dividends or when a company dissolves.

To *diversify* is to put your money in many different companies' stocks. Diversifying lessens the risk of having your money in just one company and protects you from catastrophic changes in one company ruining your investment. When you hold stocks in many companies, one company's poor performance is offset by others doing well, thereby keeping your investment portfolio in good shape.

Stock Certificates

Decades ago, when you bought a share of stock, you received a paper certificate that stated the investor's name, number of shares, and other important information. Today, paper certificates are impractical, as transactions are handled electronically. About 75 percent of all electronic registrations are in the name of your brokerage firm (called *street name*).

Although you do not receive a paper certificate, you do receive periodic statements and dividend payments—if the company pays a dividend. The Securities Investor Protection Corporation (SPIC) insures your securities, up to $500,000, against the possible bankruptcy of your brokerage firm.

Corporations: Shareholder's Limited Liability

From a legal perspective, a company can be formed as a

- *proprietorship*, privately owned by one person;
- *partnership*, privately owned by a few people; or
- *corporation*, publically owned by many people or groups.

The general public does not have access to ownership in a privately owned company.

Under the law, a corporation is a separate legal entity from the shareholders, with special legal rights, responsibilities, and a unique name. A very important feature of a public corporation's stock is *limited liability*. This means that if the company loses a lawsuit and must pay a huge judgment, the company may run out of money and your stock can become worthless, but as a shareholder your personal assets are not at risk of being taken away. Your liability is limited.

Dividends

When companies earn profits, they either retain them for future use or distribute them to shareholders in the form of a dividend. A company is not obligated to pay a dividend, so when the company needs its cash, it can keep it. The company's board of directors makes the decision whether to issue a dividend or not, when to distribute the dividend, how much the dividend will be, and in what form it will be delivered—usually cash or company stock. Investors are attracted to companies that have a good history of paying dividends. A shareholder's profit can come from a combination of dividends received and increased stock prices. When a board declares a dividend of $0.30 per share and you own 100 shares, you will get a check for $30 (100 × $0.30).

How to Buy or Sell Stocks

You can purchase stock in one of the following three ways:

1. *Directly from the company.* You can buy a single share of stock from many corporations through online service companies, such as OneShare.com. Several companies also offer direct stock-purchase plans. In most cases, you agree to automatic withdrawals from your checking account and the company purchases shares for you and charges your account monthly. Many company websites have a "contact us" or "investor relations" button to help you get things started. Also, some companies offer a dividend reinvestment plan (DRIP). These plans allow you to send a check and they'll purchase fractional shares (less than one) for you. Usually you have to already own at least one share to enroll.

2. *Directly from a stockbroker.* Stockbrokers are members of a stock-brokerage firm, and their primary roles are to help investors put their money in and take it out of the stock market and guide investors by providing accurate information to help maximize their stock-market financial returns. Stock-brokerage firms can offer their services through traditional offices or through the Internet. The fee you pay them, called a *commission*, can range from five dollars to several hundred dollars. Once you open an account with a brokerage firm, you can begin investing money by purchasing stocks and other investments like bonds and mutual funds.

3. *Directly from a person or organization.* You can buy a single share of stock directly from individuals or organizations. If they have a certificate, they can sign it just like a car title and give it to you. If there is no certificate, it is probably wise not to do the deal, because of the risk that they are not real owners.

Types of Investors

Investors in stocks are usually categorized as *growth* or *value*. You can be both, but most investors fall into one category or the other. The categories are not opposites, just different strategies. Here is a list of characteristics for growth and value stocks; they're not comprehensive lists, but they are a good start. Which group are you in?

Growth-Investing Characteristics

- Companies don't pay dividends.
- Growth in revenue and profit are higher than average growth.
- Operations are expanding.
- There is a holding period determined by the growth of the company.

Value-Investing Characteristics

- Companies pay dividends
- Earnings per share are higher than average.
- Stocks are in solid industries, but maybe not sexy ones.
- The holding period is longer than for growth stocks.

When to Sell

With today's stock markets, it is easy to sell a stock any time you want. Reasons to sell are usually either personal or market-driven. Before you sell, be sure to review the best information (accurate, timely, comprehensive, relevant), but in the end it is acceptable to conclude a stock isn't working for you anymore and move on.

Personal Reasons

Reasons like the following reflect personal preferences and are separate from market-driven factors:

- *You've reached your goals.* You are at a key lifetime moment (buying a home, retirement) and it is time to liquidate your investment.
- *The risk is too high.* You wanted a steady growth company but got one that changes a lot, so you'll sell it and buy something that suits your comfort level.
- *You need cash.* Unplanned expenses arise, so you'll sell an underperforming stock for cash and potential tax benefits.
- *Moral or ethical conflicts have arisen.* The company no longer represents your views on environmental and social issues, or meets your moral and religious standards. If these issues are important to you, you'll act.

Market-Driven Reasons

Other reasons for selling reflect conditions beyond your immediate control that impact your personal investment rate of return, such as the following:

- *Significant company changes have taken place.* The company is no longer the company you bought because of factors like new leadership, unfavorable court judgment, or not developing new products.
- *The stock has dropped by X percent.* If prices are falling by a set amount, say 8 percent, you'll sell for a small loss to ensure that it doesn't become a bigger loss.
- *The stock is overvalued.* Buy low and sell high. When stocks have made gains that can't be sustained, it's time to sell and realize your gains. Decide and don't look back. The stock may continue to go up for a while, but that's okay too, since you made an acceptable profit already.
- *Your portfolio needs balancing*: Many investors diversify investments between cash, bonds, and stocks. If your stock holdings represent more than a certain percentage (like 60 percent) of all your investments, you need to sell and put the money into a different type of investment. Be sure to hold your stocks long enough to qualify for long-term capital-gains tax treatment, however.

Calculate Profit and Rate of Return

After you sell your stock, how much money did you make? To figure that out, you'll need to know your cost basis, which is usually the sum of the original purchase price plus commissions and less any return of capital during the time you held the investment. Compare your cost basis to your sale proceeds, and the difference represents your profit on that investment. To calculate your profit and rate of return, use these formulas:

- *Profit* equals sales proceeds (sale price less commissions plus dividends received) minus cost basis (original purchase price plus commissions).
- *Rate of return* equals profit divided by cost basis.

Exercise

Stock Profits

You bought eighty shares of stock at $32 each plus a $75 commission and sold them for $47 each and a $75 commission. You also received three dividends of $1.28, $1.30, and $1.34 per share. What is the profit and rate of return?

See appendix 1, "Exercises," for the answer.

How Stock Prices Change with the Stock Market

When you give $1,000 to a stockbroker (or mutual fund) to invest in a stock, the broker will buy as many shares as the $1,000 will cover in your name. You can buy 50 shares of a stock costing $20 per share for $1,000 (ignore commissions and taxes for this illustration). As long as the price of $20 per share doesn't change, you still have access to $1,000 if you want to sell. You are also a part (probably a very small part) owner of the company. Now consider what happens when the stock price moves down, resulting in low rates of return or even loss of principal:

- Other investors who own the stock become concerned about the company's future. They want to sell their shares and move on to another investment. If enough other stockholders sell their shares, the price of the stock continues to drop. It drops because finding buyers becomes more difficult; when you have more sellers than buyers, the sellers must lower their price to attract buyers.

- If you decide to sell your fifty shares, you will have to accept what the market is willing to pay, and that may be less than you originally paid. If the current market price is $15 per share, that's what you will receive if you decide to sell (again, ignoring commissions and such).
- What happened to that $5 per share or $250 dollars you won't be receiving? (Fifty shares at $15 per share equals $750, or a loss to you of $250). No one got that $5 per share or $250. It simply vanished, because the price you had to offer a buyer to complete the sale was $5 per share less than you paid. You take a loss in your investment, and that's the big difference between saving and investing: the potential for loss.

The scenario changes when stock prices move up, resulting in high rates of return:

- Other investors decide the stock was a good buy. To induce owners to sell, buyers raise the price they are willing to pay. More buyers than sellers means the price per share continues to rise as buyers try to coax owners to sell.
- If the price goes to $25 per share, your $1,000 original investment is now worth $1,250, and that's what you will receive if you decide to sell (again, ignoring commissions and such).

Company Stock Reports and Stock Terminology

There are three important reports that public companies produce to keep investors and the general public informed about their performance:

1. The *annual report* is given to all shareholders and is available for general reference by the public and prospective investors. It can be a simple 10-K or a presentation that's

more like a magazine. The report contains descriptions of the year's key events (products, markets, operations) and what's new and exciting for the future. It also contains an audited financial statement and notes.

2. *Form 10-K* is a standardized annual report that is filed with the Securities and Exchange Commission (SEC). The report contains an overview of the company, select information, a list of the senior management, a letter from the senior management, consolidated financial statements with footnotes, and an auditor's statement.

3. *Form 10-Q* is a quarterly report filed with the SEC. The report contains select information, unaudited financial statements with footnotes, and a management discussion.

Not all shares of stock are created equal; they have different attributes. Learn them and you will make better decisions.

- *Authorized shares* represent the total number of shares of stock authorized when the company was created. Only a vote by the shareholders can increase this number of shares.
- *Restricted shares* are company stock used for employee incentive and compensation plans. Restricted stockowners need permission from the SEC to sell. There is a waiting period after a company first goes public during which insiders' restricted stock is frozen. Even insiders of established companies must file with the SEC before selling their restricted stock.
- *Float shares* refers to the number of shares actually available for trade on the open market for anyone to buy.
- *Outstanding shares* include all the shares issued by the company (restricted shares plus float shares).
- *Unissued shares* are shares that companies retain in their treasury for future use. Just because a company authorizes a certain number of shares doesn't mean it must issue all of them to the public. These unissued shares are not offered to employees either.

Discussion

1. If you invest in stocks, do you expect to make more money (profit) than other investments? Why or why not?
2. How do dividends impact your profit?
3. Do you think you are more interested in value stocks or growth stocks?

Conclusion

Stock markets are secondary markets where investors can buy and sell stocks from various companies. Stay informed about current events, because they drive market changes. Diversify your stock holdings to reduce the risk of catastrophic loss from a single company. There are plenty of investing strategies out there—buy and hold, active trading, index investing, and (you've heard it before) buy low and sell high. Stockbrokers provide a valuable service, but look for lower fees. Sometimes you'll make money and sometimes you won't, so it is acceptable to conclude a stock isn't working for you anymore and move on. Over time, people usually earn more from owning stock than from leaving money in the bank, buying bonds, or making other investments.

16

SAVINGS BASICS

Today's young adults, either Generation Y or the Millennials, must learn to save early and often. Why? They will have less access to generous retirement benefits (pensions and health insurance), wait an extra year or two for social-security benefits (age 67+), be less reliant on their home for equity, and pay higher costs for raising children.

A key life lesson is to establish good savings habits now, like PYF (pay yourself first). With good habits, you'll let your money work for you rather than you working for your money. Setting up an automated or scheduled deposit to your savings account can really help you save. You can change the amount, frequency, and transfer date whenever you want.

You've got the ability to manage through difficult times and plentiful times by making smart money decisions now. Balance risk and return, and harness the power of the time value of money for your direct benefit.

Exercise

Get an Early Start on Savings

Consider two adults, age twenty-two, with opposite saving habits. Adult A saves $2,000 a year for ten years (total of $20,000) and then has no additional savings for the next forty years. Adult B saves nothing for the first ten years and then saves $2,000 a year for the next forty years (total of $80,000). Each investor has a 9 percent annual return on the savings/investments. When they both reach seventy-two, who will have more money? Why? Which of these two would you rather be?

See appendix 1, "Exercises," for the answer.

Loan the Bank Your Money

By depositing your money in a bank, you are actually lending your money to that institution. In return, the bank will pay you for the use of your money. This is called *interest income*, and it is usually measured as a percentage on an annual basis. The more you loan the bank and the longer you let the bank use it, the higher the interest rate and the more interest income the bank will pay you. This relationship between time, money, and interest is called the *time value of money.*

A savings account can be a good place to keep your money in certain situations, like setting aside funds for a purchase in the next few months or for an unexpected expense. At some banks, you can tie a savings account to a checking account. This gives you a nice backup to your checking account in case you need to transfer money into it.

If you have a sum of money to invest but are not sure how you want to invest it yet, a savings account is a smart place to hold it. Keep it in a checking account, and you may be tempted to spend it. With a savings account, you can at least make a small amount in interest while you decide how to invest your money.

What's Needed to Open an Account?

- *Personal identification*: driver's license, passport, social-security card
- *Money to deposit*: usually a small minimum balance, such as ten dollars
- *Signature card*: Fill out all information and sign it in the presence of a witness (bank employee). The bank keeps this card on file to authenticate your signature regarding certain transactions.

Types of Savings Accounts

Find out what savings opportunities your bank offers, and select the one that works best for you.

Regular Savings or Passbook Account

With this type of account, the bank may give you a booklet that you use to record deposits, withdrawals, and interest. These savings accounts usually have few fees, a low or no minimum balance requirement, and a low interest rate. It is easy to access your money without penalties, and deposited funds are insured by the Federal Deposit Insurance Corporation (FDIC) up to $100,000—or $250,000 for retirement accounts.

Certificates of Deposit (CDs)

These accounts used to be known as high-yield savings accounts, but with today's low interest rates, there is nothing "high yield" about them. You keep your money in for a fixed period of time—such as three months or five years—and receive a higher interest rate. However, there are penalties for early withdrawal, and you usually can't use checks with this type of savings account, although you may be able to link it to your checking account for deposits and withdrawals. This type of savings account is also FDIC-insured.

Health Savings Account (HSA)

Employers may provide these accounts for tax-deductible money contributions from employees. Once you contribute money to the HSA, you can use it to pay for qualified medical expenses for yourself, your spouse, or your dependents now, or save and grow the balance to use later in life or in retirement—all taxfree.

Individual Retirement Account (IRA)

Interest earned is tax-free until you withdraw it after age 59. There are penalties for withdrawing your money earlier.

Good Savings Habits

With good habits, you'll let your money work for you rather than you working for your money. Commit to doing these all the time. The benefits are great.

- *Pay yourself first.* No matter what your paycheck or allowance is, deposit a set amount into a savings account or investment before using any of your money for anything else. It's your reward for working hard.
- *Contribute regularly.* Make it a habit throughout your whole life. Even little deposits add up. Did you know $13.10 deposited each week for fifty years equals $34,000, but at 10 percent interest it will yield $1 million? Now that's saving!
- *Collect pocket change.* At the end of each day, put your loose coins into a container. Once a month, deposit them into your savings account.
- *Surprise money means surprise savings.* Put all or a portion of unexpected money into savings and accelerate your savings success. This includes things like birthday or graduation gifts.

Exercise

Rule of 72

A simple way to figure out how long it will take your money to double at a given interest rate is to divide 72 by the interest rate. The answer is roughly the number of years it will take to double your investment. Examples:

2 percent interest rate = $\dfrac{72}{2}$ = 36 years

6 percent interest rate = $\dfrac{72}{6}$ = _____ years

10 percent interest rate = $\dfrac{72}{10}$ = _____ years

It also works in reverse. This equation will tell you what interest rate you need to earn to double your money in a certain number of years. Examples:

6 years = $\dfrac{72}{6}$ = 12 percent interest rate

8 years = $\dfrac{72}{8}$ = _____ percent interest rate

10 years = $\dfrac{72}{10}$ = _____ percent interest rate

If you put $3,000 in an investment earning 10 percent a year at age 19, how many times must your money double to have $1 million? How old will you be?

See appendix 1, "Exercises," for the answer.

Savings versus Investment

What's the difference between saving and investing? Basically, saving money is an *event.* You put money aside on a regular basis. You spend less money than you earn and put the rest into the bank. This should be a part of your monthly budget. Investing money, on the other hand, is a *process*. Money from current and previous years is set aside for future benefit, to achieve long-term monetary growth.

For many people, savings involves a safe but low-interest-bearing savings account. For higher rates of return, you need other investments, like mutual funds or stocks. Then your investments will make more each month than you are contributing. This is when you really begin to grow your wealth.

When you begin to build wealth, it's important to spread your risk and keep easy access to your emergency money. You don't need to have twenty mutual funds, but three or four is a good start. Additionally, you may consider investing in real estate for a good passive source of income. Real estate also tends to rise in value over time. However, do not do this until you are ready to purchase in cash and have cash flow for any repairs or other expenses involved with the properties.

This plan is fairly straightforward, but it will not begin to work until you spend less than you earn and focus on getting out of debt. Start budgeting, and then you can begin saving and investing effectively. Your net worth is determined by subtracting your debt from your assets. If you accumulate debt as fast as you save and invest, then you are not going to come out ahead.

Outcomes for savings and investment are driven by completely different influences. If you know you will need your money within five years, you should consider putting it in savings instruments. If you can wait more than five years and are willing to risk suffering a loss, investing potentially pays much more than saving.

Savings

No one knows what the future will bring, but that doesn't mean you can't be prepared for it. Knowing you have money in the bank to fund your lifestyle or retirement provides peace of mind. No matter what stage in life you're at, the sooner you start saving, the longer your money has to grow.

If you regularly put money into a bank account insured by the FDIC, you can count on the money being there when you need it. No depositor has lost money in any federally insured savings account within the insurance limits (usually $250,000 per account). Even if the bank fails, the worst that can happen is you may lose some earned interest, but you will still get your deposited money back. This safety is one of the reasons bank interest rates are usually low. US Treasury issues, such as bonds, notes, and bills—which are safer than bank deposits—pay even lower interest rates.

Investing

When you deposit money in a savings account, you do not own a small part of the bank, in the way an investor owns a small part of a company. You will never make more than the stated interest rate on a savings instrument, whereas an investment offers the potential—though not the guarantee—that you will earn a higher rate of return. Investors recognize that it takes time to earn big bucks, so they are patient. In most years, the earnings or losses are bigger than what you would earn or lose in a savings account. With this volatile earnings risk, you can receive higher interest rates. Withdrawing your money is more difficult, but it can be done.

The uncertainty of future earnings is called *earnings risk*, and you will expect to earn more interest than with a safer alternative, such as a savings account. This is the principle of *risk and return*. Note that the FDIC does not insure money invested in stocks, bonds, mutual funds, life-insurance policies, annuities, or municipal securities, even if these investments are purchased at an insured bank.

Thinking Long-Term

A healthy retirement life is a long-term event, but compared to the baby boomers before them, today's Generation X-ers or Millennials will need to save considerably more to make up for less support from employers and the government. To retire at age seventy, you'll need to save about $1 million dollars. This requires both saving and investing. Get started now, and let time and the power of compound interest help you. Follow your personal budget and deploy good financial habits. Here are a few to start with:

- *Take advantage of employer help.* Maximize employer contributions to retirement plans. If your company has no such program, contribute to a personal IRA.

- *Minimize investment fees and expenses* to grow your nest egg faster.

- *Set up direct deposit.* Payroll deduction is the easiest way to save, so have a portion of each paycheck automatically deposited into a 401(k), IRA, savings account, or investment account.

- *Don't spend your savings early.* Once you begin to build a nest egg, try not to spend any of it before retirement. Maximize social security by contributing for thirty-five years and waiting for full benefits.

Don't plan on retiring at sixty-five. Your generation will live longer. A male born in 1980 should plan for at least a 19.3-year retirement, after the higher retirement age of sixty-seven. For women, the average projected length of retirement is 21.2 years.

Saving $1 Million Dollars

Getting to $1 million will take some effort, but you can do it when you start saving early. A twenty-five-year-old will need to save about $90 per week, and will get there in fifty years, assuming a 5 percent annual return. Take advantage of help from your employer, if it is available to you. Retirement-account contributions from your employer will make it much easier to hit your retirement savings goal. If your employer matches your 401(k) contributions with $2,000 per year, you'll need to save only $50 per week. That saves you $40 a week! That's having your money work for you.

Discussion

1. Do you have a savings account? What do you use it for?
2. What do you need to do to start your own "Pay Yourself First" program?
3. True or False—Save early and often is best. Why?

Conclusion

There is no better time to start good savings habits than right now. Getting to $1 million will take some effort, but let time and the power of compound interest help you. Be sure to follow your personal budget and deploy good financial habits. Establish a relationship with a bank that will keep your money safe, pay yourself first through payroll deductions, learn how to invest for long-term wealth with higher financial returns, and live within your means. Make your money work for you.

Part Four

CHANGE YOUR FINANCIAL HABITS AND ENJOY LIFE

Why do we waste money?

We don't do it on purpose, but we all waste money at times. Even if you're the most money-savvy person on the block, you might still be wasting your money and not even realize you're doing it.

To build wealth and reach financial independence, you simply need to spend less than you earn. It is an easy concept to understand, but why is it so difficult to follow? To answer this question, you need to examine the roots of overspending and learn to avoid wasting money by looking at the mistakes of others.

The following chapters will guide you through the shift of your behavior from bad money habits to good ones, and you will successfully navigate this transition to financial independence. All you have to do is know your money. So let's get started—first with overspending and bad money habits, and then with good money habits that will let you fully enjoy life. After that, we'll take a look at the lessons you've learned throughout this book so you can refer to them often as you establish your financial independence.

17

SHIFT FROM BAD TO GREAT MONEY HABITS

When you know what factors drive your spending, you can fight back and save money so that you can spend less than you earn. Next, change your behavior so you shift away from bad money habits and toward great money habits.

Key Roots of Overspending

The following are some key roots of overspending:

1. *Easy access to credit.* It feels like free money when you get a new $2,000 credit limit, and it doesn't feel like you're spending because it doesn't look like cash. Just swipe your card and the cash is gone. The problem is, when you use the card for things you don't have the cash to pay for, you focus on small monthly payments and not on the total purchase price.
2. *Easy access to all your cash.* No more trips to the bank, now you have ATMs, checking accounts, credit and debit cards. You are never far away from your money. It's easy to waste your money, so be sure to only bring with you what you need.

3. *Giving in to temptation.* Everybody loves going out and having fun, but this is usually not in your financial best interest. Spending to feel good is okay as long as you don't go overboard. Set aside some "fun money," but if you can't afford it, don't cave in.
4. *Chasing a Higher Lifestyle.* At times, we all want more than what we have. Live within your means. If your friends have more money than you, be courteous, but let them know that you have limited resources but you value their friendship.

Use Cash to Keep Spending Under Control

The convenience of credit and debit cards makes spending easy ... just the way the sellers want it to be. You must treat cash and credit the same—a dollar of plastic has the same value as a dollar of cash. I encourage you to take a week or two and give this a try to see what effect it has on your everyday spending. Before your start, create a budget for how much cash money you will need throughout the week. If you regularly buy lunch out, count that, or if you stop for coffee on the way to work be sure to include that as well. Start the week by putting the budgeted cash in your pocket.

After one week, how did you do? Did you find that you had money left over, or did you have to pack a sack lunch on Friday because you spent your last dollar on Thursday? Regardless of the outcome, you now have a very real sense of where your money is going throughout the week. Using cash can help you regain control of spending.

Avoid Money-Wasting Activities

It is so hard to earn enough money, so why do we waste so much of it? To help you identify how you might be wasting your money, here is my opposite of a to-do list—it's a don't-do list.

- *Buy things you just don't need.* You didn't really need every season of *The Office* on DVD or front-row tickets to see Beyoncé or that Italian leather handbag. But you wanted them, and who cares how much they cost? (Solution: Remind yourself about needs versus wants.)

- *Pay full price ... for everything.* Buy new, not used. Sales? Coupons? Who needs these when they shop? (Solution: Research good deals using resources like *Consumers Digest*, opinions, online coupons, and store sales).

- *Don't mind those extra fees.* Need cash? For convenience, use an ATM from another bank that charges you an extra five dollars to take out that twenty-dollar bill. Rent a movie lately? Take it back two weeks late. Have a credit card? Pay the bill ten days after it's due. You'll be broke in no time. (Solution: Stay organized to pay bills on time, and take cash out for the week versus just two days).

- *Buy on impulse.* Sure, you just got to have it, and you don't need to make another trip. (Solution: Ask yourself, if it were full price, would you still buy it? If no, then you don't need it.)

- *Sign without reading the fine print.* You trust that you'll be paying exactly what they told you, and you'll get exactly what you paid for. No one would ever try to pull a fast one on you! (Solution: Read every word of a document before you sign, and negotiate.)

- *Skimp on car maintenance.* Don't bother to get the oil changed regularly or tires rotated or a regular tune-up. It runs fine. You'd rather just wait until something breaks completely, so you can spend an extra $900 to fix it. (Solution: Prevention helps avoid catastrophic events.)

- *Buy bulk for just one person.* If you live alone, and you don't have a family of five to feed, ten gallons of milk for $10 is no longer a great deal. (Solution: Just buy the quantity you need [i.e., quart of milk] when you need it).

- *Upgrade when you don't really need to.* Bigger is better and worth the extra cost, right? That two-gallon soda at the movie theater is only fifty cents more than the more sensible medium size soda—what a bargain! And every telephone feature known to man for only $49 a month is a steal, even though you don't know what half of the features are for and you never use them anyway. (Solution: Know what you really need.)

- *Buy extended warranties.* Things break, right? It's important to protect those pricey gadgets. (Solution: It's better to protect your investment from the get-go by purchasing big-ticket items with a major credit card that doubles the manufacturer's warranty for free. Given the rapid depreciation of electronics, it usually makes more sense to replace them after that free warranty wears off than spend money on repairs or additional warranties.)

- *Don't take it back.* You don't have time to return that shirt that had a hole in it that you didn't see when you tried it on. Or those headphones that broke the moment you opened the package. Or the beauty lotion that caused hives when you put it on. You'd rather just leave them sit in your closet or in your drawer and never get used. You'll just go buy another one. (Solution: Take it back and get that refund.)

- *Join and subscribe when you know better.* You have that gym membership, but you've only been once. You have fifteen magazine subscriptions and stacks of magazines you've never read. These things are good to have, though. (Solution: Know what you really need).

- *Text-message your heart out.* Pay the lowest monthly phone charge to save money, but then text to your heart's content regardless of the texting limit your wireless plan provides. (Solution: Match your phone plan to what you need.)

You Can Save $75,000

How hard is it to save $75,000 in your twenties? When you add it up, it is really amazing how you can really put away some big dollars while you are young. During the two years you're in college in your twenties, the following strategies will help you start saving:

- *Don't have a car.* Ride a bike or make friends with someone who has a car, and save $5,000 a year = $10,000 for two years.
- *Share a room.* Save $500 per month = $12,000 for two years.

Then, for the eight years after college, try these strategies:

- *Drive responsibly.* Speeding tickets average $150, and with a few tickets, your auto insurance cost goes up $300 a year. Drive slower and your eight-year savings = $2,700.
- *Modify your gym membership.* Unused gym memberships cost $500 a year. Try six months a year at $40/month and your eight-year savings = $2,000.
- *Choose a more modest car.* A luxury car is $53,000 and an SUV is $31,500. Add 10 percent more for taxes and fees, and save $23,650 with the SUV. Do it again after four years, so with two vehicles over eight years, your savings = $47,300.
- *Avoid extra premium cable and digital TV packages.* Save $30/month, and your eight-year savings = $2,880.
- *Don't constantly upgrade.* New high-tech gadgets come out every year for $200+. Skip a year and your eight-year savings = $800.

Total money saved over ten years exceeds $77,000, and you still had a car, went to the gym, fed your pet, saw movies on TV, and stayed out of debt.

Exercise

Wasting Money

You'd be surprised how fast small expenses add up to a big waste. Fill in the table below to see what you waste in one year.

Item	Price	Buy Often	Cost/Year
ATM fees	$3.00	2 per week	$312
Gourmet coffee	$4.00	Weekly	$208
Bag potato chips		Weekly	
Bottle soda		Weekly	
Buying lunch vs. bringing		10 per month	
Pizza delivery (+tip)		2 per month	
Excess cell-phone text and data usage fees		Monthly	
Lottery tickets		Weekly	
TOTAL			$

See appendix 1, "Exercises," for the answer.

Common Bad Money Habits

Avoiding these actions may seem like common sense, but mistakes are easy to make and we all fail to see how little things add up. Bad habits are hard to correct. They are listed here so you can avoid all of them.

- Be in no hurry to open your bills when they arrive.
- Bounce checks.
- Budget for the short term.
- Carry sizeable balances on credit cards.
- Count on social security to fund your retirement.
- Don't save for retirement, even if it means losing employer's matching contributions.
- Eat unhealthily.
- Fail to cultivate your dreams.
- Fail to develop good savings habits.
- Fail to pay debt obligations.
- Fail to see how little things add up.
- Fall victim to spending traps.
- Get emotional about your investments and hold them for too long.
- Have inadequate insurance coverage.
- Ignore interest rates.
- Ignore your credit score.
- Invest in schemes to make quick returns.
- Live for today and worry about paying for it tomorrow.
- Overspend on housing.
- Overspend on gifts.
- Pay minimum balance due on credit cards.
- Pay off cheaper loans first.
- Pay everyone else first and save "what's left over."
- Save nothing in your early years.
- Spend without a budget.
- Tend to minimize the impact of debt.
- Try to beat short-term stock-market behavior.
- Underestimate tax bills.
- Use credit cards for impulse buys.
- Wait to invest when you have extra money.

Great Money Habits to Help You Fully Enjoy Life

It's essential to know how important your early adult years are when it comes to your financial future. Your focus is on career building, paying rent, and starting personal relationships. However, it is a common misconception that managing your money wisely is too complex or means that you cannot have any fun now.

Today's generation of young adults will face very different challenges when compared to their parents. But there is a lot to be learned from the mistakes of others, and you can apply these great money habits in your life right now. They're all within your ability. Use them to establish a strong financial foundation that will enable you to fully enjoy life. Here they are in alphabetic order, because all are important:

1. *Build an emergency savings fund.* Set aside an amount equivalent to six months of take-home pay as a safety net to handle life's unplanned difficulties.
2. *Create a budget and revise it regularly.* Set realistic spending goals, track results, and adjust your habits and budget values as life changes.
3. *Develop good shopping skills.* Learn how to plan your purchases and take advantage of discounts to reduce costs.
4. *Discuss money issues with confidence.* Money is an issue that never goes away, and you'll need to discuss things with others, both good and bad. Commit yourself to know your money, understand financial fundamentals for daily living, avoid pitfalls, and have the confidence to share money ideas and work out money problems. This builds healthy relationships with your money and key people in your life.
5. *Diversify your investments.* Reduce your risk of a catastrophic loss from a single investment.
6. *Don't be house rich but cash poor.* Housing is often your number-one biggest expense. Keep housing-related costs

to no more than 36 percent of income if possible. Upgrade your home after your nonhousing debt is paid off. You'll have more money for other things in life

7. *Give to others.* Learn to enjoy helping others by giving your time, talent, and treasure. It keeps you aware of your blessings and the needs of others.
8. *Insurance can protect your assets.* Avoid the cost of catastrophic problems through good insurance programs that meet your needs. This may include medical, life, auto, home, and business.
9. *Live within your means.* Spend no more than what you earn.
10. *Maintain a high credit score.* Good creditworthiness opens doors for lower cost of borrowing. Scores of 700 or higher are best. Always pay your credit-card balance in full every month to eliminate minimum payments, which are a financial trap.
11. *Maintain a strong record-keeping system.* With good records at your fingertips you will have available the information you need to make smart decisions. Keep it in a safe place.
12. *Minimize your debt.* Borrowing money makes the things you buy more expensive. Loans benefit the lender, not the borrower, as debt is designed to grow quickly (through interest and penalty fees). Prioritize debt payments to pay down the highest-interest-rate debt first. Strive to keep total monthly debt payments to less than 15 percent of your monthly income, excluding housing.
13. *Minimize your taxes.* Take lawful steps to reduce your tax obligation so you can keep more of your money.
14. *Negotiate your salary.* Keep track of your working accomplishments and value to your employer. When things get out of balance, confront your employer in a professional manner with "value facts." If necessary, look for another job, because what you earn earlier in life makes a big difference in lifetime earnings.
15. *Pay yourself first.* Reward yourself for your hard work and then pay others.

16. *Start retirement savings early.* As a young adult, you have the advantage of time, so continue saving each year for best results. Compound interest income makes your money work for you.

17. *Take advantage of employer savings contributions.* It's free money, so ensure your contributions are enough to get the maximum employer contribution. As a bonus, your contributions may reduce your current-year taxes as well.

Discussion

1. Is it easier to spend cash or use a debit/credit card? Why?
2. Does spending money make you feel better?
3. What can you to do spend less without feeling left out with your friends?
4. What is a good impulse-buying attitude?
5. Do you think you can pursue the sixteen good money habits and still have fun? Why or why not?

Conclusion

Everybody loves going out and having fun, but too much of that hurts your financial ambitions. Learn about your personal spending habits, pay cash whenever possible, and soon you'll stop wasting your money. To reach financial independence, you simply need to adopt key objectives that let you enjoy life regardless of how much money you earn. Make a commitment to learn and implement the good money habits.

18

CHAPTER MESSAGES

There is a lot to learn, but no matter what your starting point is, get to know your money. You have a higher net worth when you save more and owe less, and with a higher net worth you can afford a higher standard of living. The good life comes when your money is working for you rather than you working for your money. It comes when your savings increase as your income increases. Now let's review the key messages from each topic, and the list of great money habits you should incorporate into your life.

Key Messages from Each Topic

Each chapter has a lot of detail, but this list will remind you of the key points to remember. I'm listing them here in alphabetical order rather than by chapter number for your reference.

- *Apartment Basics* (chapter 1): Before you sign a lease or rental agreement, think about what you really need in your new home and only make a financial commitment you can afford. "Know your money" means live within your means. You can do this by keeping your total housing costs under 36 percent of your income. Don't start out being house rich but cash poor. Your first apartment isn't going to be perfect, so know what things you can skip for now, and when you earn more income, you can move up to a better apartment with your next lease.

- *Auto-Insurance Basics* (chapter 2): Driving is a privilege, not a right. As a smart vehicle owner, you will obtain the right auto insurance to ensure the safety of you, your car, and your passengers, and also safeguard your personal assets from lawsuits. Young drivers are higher risk because they cause more accidents, so obey the law (speed, drinking, texting). Remember, you are financially responsible for damages when you loan your car, so try not to loan it, especially to high-risk drivers. Shop regularly for the best insurance coverage and fees; premiums can be reduced as you get older (over twenty-five) and become a safer and more experienced driver.

- *Budget Basics* (chapter 12): A budget is the key tool for a solid financial foundation. It increases your awareness of how and where you spend your money and helps guide your spending toward the things that are most important to you. Compare your budget versus actual spending at least once year so you can make adjustments and set new goals. Once you know where your money goes, you will make smart decisions and begin to save money. If you fail to make adjustments, then your money will likely control you. Always aspire to know your money—which means to live within your means—and you will avoid many money problems throughout your life. You can do this!

- *Checking-Account Basics* (chapter 6): Checking accounts are a convenient way to transfer funds (pay bills, deposit money) to others. Your check is not legal until you sign it. Poor use of the account hurts your credit rating, as bounced checks are considered a key predictor of future credit problems. Store your checks in a safe place, and if you lose them, notify your bank immediately. Knowing your money means regularly balancing your checkbook. It's easy to do, and when you can explain the money difference between your check register value and your bank statement value at the end of the month, then your account is in balance.

- *Credit-Card Basics* (chapter 7): Your credit-card usage is linked to your credit rating, which also has a tremendous impact on your financial life, both now and in the future. Whatever kind of card you start out with, you have it in your power to create for yourself an enviable position: a solid, clean credit history with a good credit score. Build it wisely and reap the benefits; make mistakes, and you'll be paying a penalty for many years to come. Don't charge more than you can pay, and try to pay in full so you don't face interest charges. Make sure to pay on time, even if you can't pay in full. Making a minimum payment is a bad habit. Stay away from credit cards with a universal clause.

- *Credit Score and Repair* (chapter 8): Maintain a good credit history to qualify for credit when you most need it, faster, and at better interest rates and therefore lower costs. You improve your credit score by paying your bills on time; paying down your debt; applying for credit sparingly; and correcting errors. A poor score will not haunt you forever, because a score is for a point in time. As the information changes, so does your score—that is why lenders want the most current report to make the best decision. It's smart to fix errors in all three reports before you shop for a loan.

- *Debit versus Credit Cards* (chapter 9): Debit cards are convenient, with few fees, but they do not contribute to your credit history and leave your bank accounts vulnerable to fraud. Credit cards only offer you a credit option—a loan you must repay in the future—but have better fraud liability protection. In general, debit cards are best for small payments that you can easily pay in full, and you can avoid problems by comparing receipts to your bank statements each month. For most people, using both a credit and a debit card makes sense. Either way, do not spend more than what you can pay, and you'll enjoy the benefits that each card provides.

- *Federal Tax-Filing Basics* (chapter 4): Each calendar year, most US residents with earned income must pay taxes to the US government and are required to file a federal tax return (US Individual Income Tax Return, commonly known as Form 1040). You must file by April 15 of the following year. You must file a return even if you owe no tax. The government enforces the tax code through the Internal Revenue Service (IRS) by combining information from many sources to verify that the tax information you submit correctly matches the amount owed. All taxpayers are entitled to take all lawful steps to minimize their tax liability—like claiming deductions and credits. Filing a tax return with false information is a crime punishable by law, known as tax evasion.

- *Interest: Friend and Foe* (chapter 13): Interest works the same way in investments (interest income) as it does in borrowing (interest expense). Borrowing money makes the things you buy more expensive. Loans benefit the lender, not the borrower. Installment loans are a relatively safe means of borrowing, but good money habits include saving for larger purchases and not borrowing money by paying cash. The biggest obstacle to higher net worth is when you borrow too much money.

- *Introduction to Investment Options* (chapter 14): There are four key elements to determine how much money your investments will be worth: type of investment, risk (rate of return), time, and diversification. Invest early and often and the power of compounding interest will improve your rate of return. Diversify your investments to reduce the risk of catastrophic loss from a single investment. All investments vary in terms of risk, so to help you know your money, it is okay to ask others so you can gain control.

- *Introduction to the Stock Market* (chapter 15): Stock markets are secondary markets where investors can buy and sell stocks from various companies. Stay informed about current events, because they drive market changes. Diversify your stock holdings to reduce the risk of catastrophic loss from a single company. There are plenty of investing strategies out there—buy and hold, active trading, index investing, and buying low and selling high. Stockbrokers provide a valuable service, but look for lower fees. Sometimes you'll make money and sometimes you won't, so it is acceptable to conclude that a stock isn't working for you anymore and move on. Over time, people usually earn more from owning stock than from leaving money in the bank, buying bonds, or making other investments.

- *Paychecks and Payroll Taxes* (chapter 3): Payroll taxes are an obligation, but proper withholding will help you avoid a big tax bill when you file your income tax return by April 15. Be aware of the changes in the tax code each year, and change your withholding (W-4 exemptions, voluntary items) as things in your life change.

- *Paying Bills* (chapter 5): Paying bills late is very expensive, especially for credit cards. So the most important thing is to find a system that works for you. The basics of keeping your bills organized boils down to storing them in one place and paying them according to a set schedule. If you use online bill-payment methods, be sure the website is secure and that you use tough passwords and stay on top of authorized automatic payments. Don't throw old bank or financial records in the trash because paper documents can easily be used to steal your identity.

Instead, you should shred them. Lastly, it's a good idea to save select documents in support of your tax returns. Keep this information for three years, because that's how long the IRS has to audit you (and the same time frame you have to file an amended tax return).

- *Personal-Planning Basics* (chapter 11): Goals are an integral part of financial independence. If you don't have a goal, get one. Start now with goals that are meaningful to you and in line with your personal values. Stay simple, monitor your progress, and update your goals periodically. Don't waste your time or money on unnecessary things; aspire to live within your means by reducing liabilities and increasing assets to achieve your financial goals, both shortterm and long-term. Victories can be both small and large; don't forget to celebrate along the way.

- *Protect Your Financial Information* (chapter 10): Protect your personal Information and report a problem quickly. Identity theft is growing, and it can damage your credit rating for many years. Use common sense when issuing your personal information to others. Don't sign anything you don't understand. Let the bank protect your cash, be aware of scams, don't hand out your PIN number, be cautious of joint accounts, and look for secure Internet websites before you conduct any online transactions. Put in place a good record-keeping system to stay organized, and you'll have the information you need when you need it.

- *Savings Basics* (chapter 16): There is no better time to start good savings habits than right now. Getting to $1 million will take some effort, but let time and the power of compound interest help you. Be sure to follow your personal budget and deploy good financial habits. Establish a relationship with a bank that will keep your money safe, pay yourself first through payroll deductions, learn how to invest for long-term wealth with higher financial returns, and live within your means. Make your money work for you.

- *Shift from Bad to Great Money Habits* (chapter 17): Everybody loves going out and having fun, but too much of that hurts your financial ambitions. Learn about your personal spending habits, pay cash whenever possible, and soon you'll stop wasting your money. To reach financial independence, you simply need to adopt financial objectives that let you enjoy life regardless of how much money you earn. Make a commitment to learn and implement these great money habits.

Incorporate These Great Money Habits into Your Life

You can apply these great money habits in your life, they're all within your ability to do so right now. Use them to establish a strong financial foundation that will enable you to fully enjoy life. Here they are in alphabetic order, because all are important:

1. *Build an emergency savings fund.* Set aside an amount equivalent to six months of take-home pay as a safety net to handle life's unplanned difficulties.
2. *Create a budget and revise it regularly.* Set realistic spending goals, track results, and adjust your habits and budget values as life changes.
3. *Develop good shopping skills.* Learn how to plan your purchases and take advantage of discounts to reduce costs.
4. *Discuss money issues with confidence.* Money is an issue that never goes away, and you'll need to discuss things with others, both good and bad. Commit yourself to know your money, understand financial fundamentals for daily living, avoid pitfalls, and have the confidence to share money ideas and work out money problems. This builds healthy relationships with your money and key people in your life.

5. *Diversify your investments.* Reduce your risk of a catastrophic loss from a single investment.
6. *Don't be house rich but cash poor.* Housing is often your number-one biggest expense. Keep housing-related costs to no more than 36 percent of income if possible. Upgrade your home after your nonhousing debt is paid off. You'll have more money for other things in life
7. *Give to others.* Learn to enjoy helping others by giving your time, talent, and treasure. It keeps you aware of your blessings and the needs of others.
8. *Insurance can protect your assets.* Avoid the cost of catastrophic problems through good insurance programs that meet your needs. This may include medical, life, auto, home, and business.
9. *Live within your means.* Spend no more than what you earn.
10. *Maintain a high credit score.* Good creditworthiness opens doors for lower cost of borrowing. Scores of 700 or higher are best. Always pay your credit-card balance in full every month to eliminate minimum payments, which are a financial trap.
11. *Maintain a strong record-keeping system.* With good records at your fingertips you will have available the information you need to make smart decisions. Keep it in a safe place.
12. *Minimize your debt.* Borrowing money makes the things you buy more expensive. Loans benefit the lender, not the borrower, as debt is designed to grow quickly (through interest and penalty fees). Prioritize debt payments to pay down the highest-interest-rate debt first. Strive to keep total monthly debt payments to less than 15 percent of your monthly income, excluding housing.
13. *Minimize your taxes.* Take lawful steps to reduce your tax obligation so you can keep more of your money.
14. *Negotiate your salary.* Keep track of your working accomplishments and value to your employer. When things get out of balance, confront your employer in a professional manner with "value facts." If necessary,

look for another job, because what you earn earlier in life makes a big difference in lifetime earnings.

15. *Pay yourself first.* Reward yourself for your hard work and then pay others.

16. *Start retirement savings early.* As a young adult, you have the advantage of time, so continue saving each year for best results. Compound interest income makes your money work for you.

17. *Take advantage of employer savings contributions.* It's free money, so ensure your contributions are enough to get the maximum employer contribution. As a bonus, your contributions may reduce your current-year taxes as well.

Epilogue

LET THE JOURNEY BEGIN

It's only money!

Financial independence is a great goal for today's generation of young adults. This book has shared many ideas to help you make smart financial decisions for daily living. There is a romantic notion that it is easy to be young and live the good life—and that we can all afford to live it. However, life is not so romantic when we look at our cramped apartment, hand-me-down car, used furniture, old clothes, unpaid bills, and no vacation in sight. There is a lot to learn, but no matter what your starting point is, the key is to KNOW YOUR MONEY. Now you know:

- you have your own unique values and money-management habits;
- the major issue for you is not how much money you earn but how much money you spend;
- you will have a higher net worth when you save more and owe less, and with a higher net worth you can afford a higher standard of living;
- the decisions you make today will impact your life both now and in the future;

- you do not need to fear handling your money because you have the ability to control your money throughout your life's journey.

The good life comes when your money is working for you rather than you working for your money. It comes when your savings increase as your income increases. This book has shared many ideas to help you make smart financial decisions for daily living. We've covered many topics like housing, transportation, taxes, planning, credit cards, bill paying, record keeping, savings, wasting money, and shifting from bad to great money habits.

I hope this book helped you to:

- confidently discuss money issues with others;
- learn to make good financial choices;
- become more independent without being a slave to debt;
- be prepared for tough economic times (they will come at some point); and
- worry less about money and spend more time enjoying life's journey.

Plan to achieve big dreams. Now that you have the tools to get started, you can make smart decisions in both good and bad times, prepare for a financially secure future, and help others along the way. No matter what stage of life you are in, *aspire to live within your means*. No debts, no frets. Remember, you have the skills to take control of your finances. The key is to know your money.

Enjoy your financial independence and your personal life's journey, wherever it may lead you.

Appendix 1

EXERCISES

Here are the answers to select chapter exercises.

Deductible and Covered Damages

Your insurance claim is $2,000. Your policy has a deductible of $750. Therefore, the policy payment for covered damages is $2,000 – $750 = $1,250.

Take-Home Pay

Take-home pay is 62 percent of gross salary for both the biweekly pay period and annual earnings.

	Biweekly	# Pay Periods	Annual
Salary	$1,540	26	$40,040
- Flexible-Spending Account	($150)	26	($3,900)
- Retirement Savings Account	($75)	26	($1,950)
Net Taxable Income	$1,315	26	$34,190
- Federal Tax Withholding 25%	($329)	26	($8,548)
- State Tax Withholding 2.5%	($33)	26	($855)
Take-Home Pay	$953	26	$24,787
% of Salary	62%		62%

Tax Calculation

Balance due is a refund to you of $1,026.75.

Taxable Income	$56,600			
- Tuition and Fees	($6,000)			
- Student Loan Interest	($1,800)			
Adjusted Gross Income	$48,800			
- Standard Deduction	($6,100)			
- Exemptions	($3,900)			
Taxable Income	$38,800	$5,366.25	$6,393	($1,026.75)
		Tax Bill (owe)	Tax Withheld	Refund

Setting Goals

Revised SMART goal: "I'll save $1,000 in two months through automatic transfers from my checking account to my savings account of $125 each week. I'll reward myself with a manicure when I'm halfway there and a full-body massage when I reach my goal." Now the goal is clear, easily monitored, and has a timeline and a reward—it's perfect.

Credit-Card Terms Explained

There is a lot of information available online at:

- CreditCards.com (http://www.creditcards.com/glossary/a-terms.php),
- MainStreet.com (http://www.mainstreet.com/slideshow/moneyinvesting/credit/debt/10-credit-card-terms-explained),
- CreditCardDiva.com (http://www.creditcarddiva.com/cards/financial-terms.shtml).

Get familiar with credit-card terminology; look up the following terms:

Annual fee
Annual percentage rate (APR)
Authorized user
Balance transfer
Billing cycle
Cash advance
Card member agreement
Charge-back
Credit line
Due date
Finance charge
Fixed rate (or fixed APR)
Grace period
Late payment fee
Minimum finance charge
Minimum payment
Over-limit fee
Secured credit cards
Terms and conditions
Unsecured credit cards
Variable interest rate

Create a Budget

This suggested format lets you bridge key information from your paycheck (for monthly income) to your spending (monthly expenses). Feel free to add, delete, or change lines to make it more personal for your situation.

PREPARE A BUDGET

	Monthly	x 12 =	Annual
INCOME			
Salary	$ -		$ -
Other Income	$ -		$ -
Interest Income	$ -		$ -
Gross Income	$ -		$ -

Payroll Taxes	$ -	$ -
Pretax Deductions	$ -	$ -
Benefit Deductions	$ -	$ -
Other Deductions	$ -	$ -
Deductions	$ -	$ -
Net Cash Income	$ -	$ -

EXPENSES
Home

Mortgage or Rent	$ -	$ -
Property Taxes	$ -	$ -
Insurance - Home/Renters	$ -	$ -
Home Repair	$ -	$ -
Home Improvements	$ -	$ -

Utilities

Gas	$ -	$ -
Electric	$ -	$ -
Water	$ -	$ -
Cable	$ -	$ -
Telephone	$ -	$ -

Debts

Credit Cards	$ -	$ -
Student Loans	$ -	$ -
Other Loans	$ -	$ -

Transportation

Auto Maintenance	$ -	$ -
Auto - Fuel	$ -	$ -
Insurance Auto	$ -	$ -
Other Transportation (Bus, Train)	$ -	$ -

Food

| Groceries | $ - | $ - |
| Dining | $ - | $ - |

Health

Insurance Medical	$ -	$ -
Recreation	$ -	$ -
Health Club	$ -	$ -

Entertainment

Hobbies	$ -	$ -
Entertainment - Movies, Videos	$ -	$ -
Recreation	$ -	$ -
Subscriptions	$ -	$ -
Vacation Travel	$ -	$ -

Personal Items

Clothing	$ -	$ -
Dry Cleaning	$ -	$ -
Gifts	$ -	$ -
Grooming	$ -	$ -
Household	$ -	$ -
Pets -Food & Vet	$ -	$ -

Investments / Savings

Education	$ -	$ -
Insurance Life	$ -	$ -
Savings	$ -	$ -
Investments	$ -	$ -

Charity

	$ -	$ -

Other Items

Miscellaneous	$ -	$ -
Office Supplies	$ -	$ -
Postage	$ -	$ -
Other	$ -	$ -
Other	$ -	$ -
Total Expenses	$ -	$ -
Net Cash	$ -	$ -

Simple versus Compound Interest

The difference in interest earned is $250 (simple) versus $277 (compound) or $27 more for compound interest. Here are the updated tables:

Simple	Year 1	Year 2	Year 3	Year 4	Year 5
Base Investment	$1,000	$1,000	$1,000	$1,000	$1,000
Interest	$50	$50	$50	$50	$50
Balance YE	$1,050	$1,100	$1,150	$1,200	$1,250

Compound	Year 1	Year 2	Year 3	Year 4	Year 5
Base Investment	$1,000	$1,050	$1,103	$1,158	$1,216
Interest	$50	$53	$55	$58	$61
Balance YE	$1,050	$1,103	$1,158	$1,216	$1,277

Car Payments

Total borrowing is $24,400 ($22,500 + $325 + $1,575) over five years (sixty monthly payments) and a 9 percent interest rate. Monthly payments are $506.50 each, times 60 = $30,386 total paid (total cost of borrowing), which includes $24,400 principal and $5,990 interest. If you paid cash, you would avoid interest expenses, saving you $5,990 or about 19.7 percent versus taking a loan.

No.	Payment Date	Beginning Balance	Payment	Principal	Interest (Monthly)	End Balance
1	6/1/14	$24,400.00	$506.50	$323.50	$183.00	$24,076.50
2	7/1/14	24,076.50	506.50	325.93	180.57	23,750.57
3	8/1/14	23,750.57	506.50	328.37	178.13	23,422.19
4	9/1/14	23,422.19	506.50	330.84	175.67	23,091.35
5	10/1/14	23,091.35	506.50	333.32	173.19	22,758.04

6	11/1/14	22,758.04	506.50	335.82	170.69	22,422.22
7	12/1/14	22,422.22	506.50	338.34	168.17	22,083.88
8	1/1/15	22,083.88	506.50	340.87	165.63	21,743.00
9	2/1/15	21,743.00	506.50	343.43	163.07	21,399.57
10	3/1/15	21,399.57	506.50	346.01	160.50	21,053.57
11	4/1/15	21,053.57	506.50	348.60	157.90	20,704.96
12	5/1/15	20,704.96	506.50	351.22	155.29	20,353.75
13	6/1/15	20,353.75	506.50	353.85	152.65	19,999.90
14	7/1/15	19,999.90	506.50	356.50	150.00	19,643.39
15	8/1/15	19,643.39	506.50	359.18	147.33	19,284.21
16	9/1/15	19,284.21	506.50	361.87	144.63	18,922.34
17	10/1/15	18,922.34	506.50	364.59	141.92	18,557.76
18	11/1/15	18,557.76	506.50	367.32	139.18	18,190.43
19	12/1/15	18,190.43	506.50	370.08	136.43	17,820.36
20	1/1/16	17,820.36	506.50	372.85	133.65	17,447.51
21	2/1/16	17,447.51	506.50	375.65	130.86	17,071.86
22	3/1/16	17,071.86	506.50	378.46	128.04	16,693.40
23	4/1/16	16,693.40	506.50	381.30	125.20	16,312.09
24	5/1/16	16,312.09	506.50	384.16	122.34	15,927.93
25	6/1/16	15,927.93	506.50	387.04	119.46	15,540.88
26	7/1/16	15,540.88	506.50	389.95	116.56	15,150.94
27	8/1/16	15,150.94	506.50	392.87	113.63	14,758.06
28	9/1/16	14,758.06	506.50	395.82	110.69	14,362.25
29	10/1/16	14,362.25	506.50	398.79	107.72	13,963.46
30	11/1/16	13,963.46	506.50	401.78	104.73	13,561.68
31	12/1/16	13,561.68	506.50	404.79	101.71	13,156.89
32	1/1/17	13,156.89	506.50	407.83	98.68	12,749.06
33	2/1/17	12,749.06	506.50	410.89	95.62	12,338.18
34	3/1/17	12,338.18	506.50	413.97	92.54	11,924.21
35	4/1/17	11,924.21	506.50	417.07	89.43	11,507.14
36	5/1/17	11,507.14	506.50	420.20	86.30	11,086.94
37	6/1/17	11,086.94	506.50	423.35	83.15	10,663.59
38	7/1/17	10,663.59	506.50	426.53	79.98	10,237.06
39	8/1/17	10,237.06	506.50	429.73	76.78	9,807.33

40	9/1/17	9,807.33	506.50	432.95	73.55	9,374.38
41	10/1/17	9,374.38	506.50	436.20	70.31	8,938.19
42	11/1/17	8,938.19	506.50	439.47	67.04	8,498.72
43	12/1/17	8,498.72	506.50	442.76	63.74	8,055.96
44	1/1/18	8,055.96	506.50	446.08	60.42	7,609.87
45	2/1/18	7,609.87	506.50	449.43	57.07	7,160.44
46	3/1/18	7,160.44	506.50	452.80	53.70	6,707.64
47	4/1/18	6,707.64	506.50	456.20	50.31	6,251.45
48	5/1/18	6,251.45	506.50	459.62	46.89	5,791.83
49	6/1/18	5,791.83	506.50	463.07	43.44	5,328.76
50	7/1/18	5,328.76	506.50	466.54	39.97	4,862.22
51	8/1/18	4,862.22	506.50	470.04	36.47	4,392.19
52	9/1/18	4,392.19	506.50	473.56	32.94	3,918.62
53	10/1/18	3,918.62	506.50	477.11	29.39	3,441.51
54	11/1/18	3,441.51	506.50	480.69	25.81	2,960.82
55	12/1/18	2,960.82	506.50	484.30	22.21	2,476.52
56	1/1/19	2,476.52	506.50	487.93	18.57	1,988.59
57	2/1/19	1,988.59	506.50	491.59	14.91	1,497.00
58	3/1/19	1,497.00	506.50	495.28	11.23	1,001.72
59	4/1/19	1,001.72	506.50	498.99	7.51	502.73
60	5/1/19	502.73	502.73	498.96	3.77	0.00
TOTAL			30,386.46	24,396.23	5,990.23	

Rate of Return Calculation

Rate of return is 43.3 percent:

$$\frac{\left(\$2{,}150 \text{ final value} - \$1{,}500 \text{ original value}\right) + \$0 \text{ dividends}}{\$1{,}500 \text{ original value}} = \frac{\$650}{\$1{,}500} = 0.433 = 43.3\%$$

Stock Profits

First, add up the dividends (rounded to the nearest dollar):

- $1.28 × 80 = $102
- $1.30 × 80 = $104
- $1.35 × 80 = $108
- Total = $314

Enter this and other values in the following chart. Note that you add the first commission to your original purchase price (higher cost) but subtract the second commission from your proceeds (less income):

Item	Original Purchase	Sale Proceeds
Price per share	$32	$47
Shares	80	80
Subtotal	$2,560	$3,760
Broker commission	$75	($75)
Dividends	$0	$314
Total	$2,635	$3,999
Profit		$1,364

Profit = $1,364 ($3,999 – $2,635). Rate of return is 51.75 percent $\left(\frac{\$1,364}{\$2635}\right)$.

Employer Matching Programs

The benefits are that you save more money (get $2,500 from your employer) and reduce your tax bill by $1,875 (25% × [$5,000 + $2,500]) for a total favorable impact of $4,375. Now that's a great investment!

Rule of 72

Answer = your money must double between eight and nine times. At age eighty you will have just over $1 million.

Using the rule of 72, your money invested at a 10 percent interest will double every 7.2 years.

$$10 \text{ percent interest rate} = \frac{72}{10} = 7.2 \text{ years}$$

Starting with 3,000 at age nineteen, here's how your savings increase each year:

Age	Year	Amount		Age	Year	Amount
20	1	3,300		52	33	69,675
21	2	3,630		53	34	76,643
22	3	3,993		54	35	84,307
23	4	4,392		55	36	92,738
24	5	4,832		56	37	102,012
25	6	5,315		57	38	112,213
26	7	5,846		58	39	123,434
27	8	6,431		59	40	135,778
28	9	7,074		60	41	149,356
29	10	7,781		61	42	164,291
30	11	8,559		62	43	180,720
31	12	9,415		63	44	198,792
32	13	10,357		64	45	218,671
33	14	11,392		65	46	240,539
34	15	12,532		66	47	264,592
35	16	13,785		67	48	291,052
36	17	15,163		68	49	320,157
37	18	16,680		69	50	352,173

38	19	18,348		70	51	387,390
39	20	20,182		71	52	426,129
40	21	22,201		72	53	468,742
41	22	24,421		73	54	515,616
42	23	26,863		74	55	567,177
43	24	29,549		75	56	623,895
44	25	32,504		76	57	686,285
45	26	35,755		77	58	754,913
46	27	39,330		78	59	830,404
47	28	43,263		79	60	913,445
48	29	47,589		80	61	1,004,789
49	30	52,348		81	62	1,105,268
50	31	57,583		82	63	1,215,795
51	32	63,341		83	64	1,337,375

Get an Early Start on Savings

Who has more money? The first person with the $20,000 deposits ultimately has more money—in fact, over $300,000 more than the second person ($1,040,000 versus $736,584). Why? The power of compound interest over long periods of time makes your money work for you. Which person would you rather be? Although it's hard to do, saving a lot in your early years is better, so be like the first person.

	PERSON A			PERSON B	
Age	Deposit	Balance	Age	Deposit	Balance
22	2,000	2,180	22	-	-
23	2,000	4,556	23	-	-
24	2,000	7,146	24	-	-
25	2,000	9,969	25	-	-
26	2,000	13,047	26	-	-
27	2,000	16,401	27	-	-

28	2,000	20,057	28	-	-
29	2,000	24,042	29	-	-
30	2,000	28,386	30	-	-
31	2,000	33,121	31	-	-
32		36,101	32	2,000.00	2,180
33		39,351	33	2,000.00	4,556
34		42,892	34	2,000.00	7,146
35		46,752	35	2,000.00	9,969
36		50,960	36	2,000.00	13,047
37		55,547	37	2,000.00	16,401
38		60,546	38	2,000.00	20,057
39		65,995	39	2,000.00	24,042
40		71,934	40	2,000.00	28,386
41		78,408	41	2,000.00	33,121
42		85,465	42	2,000.00	38,281
43		93,157	43	2,000.00	43,907
44		101,541	44	2,000.00	50,038
45		110,680	45	2,000.00	56,722
46		120,641	46	2,000.00	64,007
47		131,499	47	2,000.00	71,947
48		143,334	48	2,000.00	80,603
49		156,234	49	2,000.00	90,037
50		170,295	50	2,000.00	100,320
51		185,621	51	2,000.00	111,529
52		202,327	52	2,000.00	123,747
53		220,537	53	2,000.00	137,064
54		240,385	54	2,000.00	151,580
55		262,020	55	2,000.00	167,402
56		285,601	56	2,000.00	184,648
57		311,306	57	2,000.00	203,446
58		339,323	58	2,000.00	223,936
59		369,862	59	2,000.00	246,271

60		403,150	60	2,000.00	270,615
61		439,433	61	2,000.00	297,150
62		478,982	62	2,000.00	326,074
63		522,091	63	2,000.00	357,601
64		569,079	64	2,000.00	391,965
65		620,296	65	2,000.00	429,422
66		676,123	66	2,000.00	470,249
67		736,974	67	2,000.00	514,752
68		803,301	68	2,000.00	563,260
69		875,598	69	2,000.00	616,133
70		954,402	70	2,000.00	673,765
71		1,040,298	71	2,000.00	736,584
TOTAL					
TOTAL	20,000			80,000	

Wasting Money

Little things add up. In this example, the waste is over $1,500 for the year.

ATM fees	$3.00	2 per week	$312
Gourmet coffee	$4.00	Weekly	$208
Bag potato chips	$1.00	Weekly	$52
Bottle soda	$1.50	Weekly	$78
Buying lunch vs. bringing	$3.00	10 per month	$360
Pizza delivery (+tip)	$3.00	2 per month	$72
Excess cell-phone usage fees	$20.00	Monthly	$240
Lottery tickets	$4.00	Weekly	$208
TOTAL			$1,530

Appendix 2

REFERENCE MATERIAL

Know Your Rights as a Renter

Since landlord/tenant law varies by state, to avoid problems you need to know your rights—preferably before you sign your lease or rental agreement. Here are some common renter's rights likely to be addressed in your state's law:

- The Fair Housing Act makes it illegal to deny housing to a tenant on the grounds of race, color, sex, religion, disability, family status, or national origin.
- Residential rental units should be habitable and in compliance with housing and health codes—meaning they should be structurally safe, sanitary, weatherproofed, and include adequate water, electricity, and heat. If not, you might have the legal right to break the lease.
- Landlords should make necessary repairs or maintenance in a timely manner.
- Landlords must give prior notice (typically twenty-four hours) before entering your premises and can normally only do so to make repairs or in case of an emergency.

- Landlords usually must return security deposits within fourteen to thirty days after a tenant vacates the premises, and "normal wear and tear" is not a valid reason to withhold money from your deposit.
- Landlords are usually not allowed to change the locks, shut off utilities, or evict you without notice. Eviction usually requires a court order.

Questions to Ask Your Insurance Carrier

- Can you provide a list of personal property that is typically covered without limitation (such as TV, cameras, CDs, microwaves, furniture, sports equipment, clothing, books) and personal property that is subject to limitations (computers, jewelry, antiques, art, firearms, boats)? What are the various limitations?
- What is covered as a result of damage from a natural hazard (such as vandalism, water damage from failed plumbing, hail, windstorm, smoke, explosion, vehicles, or aircraft)?
- What coverage options do you offer for hazards not included in the standard policy (earthquake, landslide, flood, nuclear)? How much does it raise the premium?
- Does my insurance cover my roommate's personal property?
- Should I take photographs of certain items now?
- Does my policy cover satellite dish or portable cellular communication equipment?
- What is the price and protection difference between "replacement cost" coverage and "depreciated cost" coverage?
- Is there medical coverage for others? If so, describe in detail.
- If my housing was damaged or destroyed, would I be covered for interim housing costs?
- Will my policy protect me for legal defense costs in the case of a lawsuit filed against me?
- Does protection include the value of wedding gifts?

Paychecks and Payroll Taxes

Withholding: Voluntary

- *Retirement Contributions to IRA or 401(k)*: These represent an opportunity to save money for future years, tax-free. Employers may provide this plan with specific participation terms and conditions unique to the company. Usually the company allows employees to save (contribute) throughout the year up to a specific percent of their salary, such as 6 percent. Many firms encourage this by providing an additional incentive, a company match—such as 35 percent—that is like free money to you. The total employee contribution may not exceed $17,500 for 2014.

- *Flexible Spending Accounts*: These are additional pretax withholding programs that you participate in voluntarily. Whatever is withheld for approved programs (such as healthcare):
  - ○ will reduce your taxable income for that calendar year, and
  - ○ must be spent for the designated purpose only.

Federal Tax-Filing Basics

Withholding: Required

Federal and state governments have the power to tax people's income through approved tax legislation. There are various kinds of taxes, such as income, investment, estate, sales, and others. Some taxes are paid on each transaction (sales tax) and some are paid annually (income tax). For payroll taxes, the employer deducts an amount from your earned income each pay period related to the amount you earned and submits the money to the government on your behalf. By withholding a little bit throughout the year you can easily pay your tax rather than have to come up with a big lump sum once a year, when you may not have that money anymore. The more you earn, the more they deduct.

The government enforces the tax code through the Internal Revenue Service (IRS) by combining information from many sources to verify that the tax information you submit correctly matches the amount owed. The US government creates the laws that define what is taxable and how much tax is owed, commonly known as the tax code. It changes every year. Employers furnish employees with annual summary statements of personal wages paid and taxes withheld on Form W-2 and any annual nonemployee compensation.

Federal Income Tax Rates 2014 (source: www.irs.gov)

Single Individuals and Head of Household: 2014

Income				
at least	but not over	tax is ...	plus % of	excess over
$0	$9,075	$0	10%	$0
$9,075	$38,900	$907.50	15%	$9,075
$38,900	$89,350	$5,081.25	25%	$38,900
$89,350	$188,350	$18,193.75	28%	$89,350
$188,350	$405,100	$45,353.75	33%	$188,350
$405,100	$406,750	$117,541.25	35%	$405,100
$406,750	all	$118,118.75	39.6%	$406,750

Married Individuals Filing Jointly or Qualifying Widow(er): 2014

Income				
at least	but not over	tax is ...	plus % of	excess over
$0	$18,150	$0	10%	$0
$18,150	$73,800	$1,815	15%	$18,150
$73,800	$148,850	$10,162.50	25%	$73,800

$148,850	$226,850	$28,925	28%	$148,850
$226,850	$405,100	$50,765	33%	$226,850
$405,100	$457,600	$109,587.50	35%	$405,100
$457,600	all	$127,962.50	39.6%	$457,600

Most Commonly Filed Federal Forms (source: www.irs.gov)

The following list includes commonly filed forms and schedules for taxpayers. Companies are not required to support all the federal income-tax forms and schedules and may not offer those forms that are less commonly used. Check the company's website to determine which forms are available for you.

Form/Schedule	Description
Form 1040	US Individual Income Tax Return
Form 1040 EZ	Income Tax Return for Single and Joint Filers with No Dependents
Schedule A	Itemized Deductions
Schedule B	Interest and Ordinary Dividends
Schedule C	Profit or Loss from Business Schedule
Schedule D	Capital Gains and Losses

Credit-Card Basics

The Credit CARD Act of 2009 is a relatively new law. The new normal for credit cards is more transparency and easier-to-understand terms, but at a higher upfront cost. Credit-card issuers and credit-industry analysts say the credit-card reform law could make credit cards more costly for all users and inaccessible for many low-income families and people with bad credit. The law likely means the return of routine annual fees, fewer rewards cards.

Millions of credit-card users will avoid retroactive interest-rate increases on existing card balances and have more time to pay their monthly bills, greater advance notice of changes in credit-card terms, and the right to opt out of significant changes in terms on their accounts. That will take the surprise out of the *gotcha* fine print and give consumers time to shop around for better deals if they don't like the new terms.

The Federal Reserve issued rules and detailed guidelines for implementing each phase of the new credit-card law. The law has fundamentally changed the way credit-card issuers market, bill, and advertise credit cards.

Highlights of the Credit CARD Act of 2009

- *Limited interest-rate hikes*: Interest-rate hikes on existing balances are allowed only under limited conditions, such as when a promotional rate ends, there is a variable rate, or the cardholder makes a late payment. Interest rates on new transactions can increase only after the first year. Significant changes in terms on accounts cannot occur without forty-five days' advance notice of the change.

- *Limited universal default*: The practice of raising interest rates on customers based on their payment records with other unrelated credit issuers, such as utility companies and other creditors, has ended for existing credit-card balances. Card issuers are still allowed to use universal default on future credit-card balances if they give at least forty-five days' advance notice of the change.

- *The right to opt out*: Consumers now have the right to opt out of or reject certain significant changes in terms on their accounts. Opting out means cardholders agree to close their accounts and pay off the balance under the old terms. They have at least five years to pay the balance.

- *Limited credit to young adults*: Credit-card issuers are banned from issuing credit cards to anyone under twenty-one unless he or she has adult cosigners on the account or can show proof of enough income to repay the card debt. Credit-card companies must stay at least a thousand feet from college campuses if they are offering free pizza or other gifts to entice students to apply for credit cards.

- *More time to pay monthly bills*: Under the credit-card law, issuers have to give account holders "a reasonable amount of time" to make payments on monthly bills. That means payments are due at least twenty-one days after bills are mailed or delivered. Consumers have complained about due dates that change without notice or are moved up, giving them less time to pay their bills and increasing the likelihood of late fees.

- *Clearer due dates and times*: Credit-card issuers are no longer able to set early-morning or other arbitrary deadlines for payments. Cutoff times set before five p.m. on payment due dates are illegal under the new credit-card law. Payments due at those times or on weekends, holidays, or whenever the card issuer is closed for business are not subject to late fees.

- *Highest-interest balances paid first*: When consumers have accounts that carry different interest rates for different types of purchases—cash advances, regular purchases, balance transfers, or ATM withdrawals—payments in excess of the minimum amount due must go to balances with higher interest rates first. Common practice in the industry had been to apply all amounts over the minimum monthly payment to the lowest-interest balances first, thus extending the time it takes to pay off higher-interest-rate balances.

- *Limits on over-limit fees*: Consumers must "opt in" to over-limit fees. Those who opt out would have their transactions rejected if they exceed their credit limit, thus avoiding over-limit fees. Fees cannot exceed the amount of overspending. For example, going twenty dollars over the limit cannot involve a fee of more than twenty dollars.

- *No more double-cycle billing*: Finance charges on outstanding credit-card balances must now be computed based on purchases made in the current cycle rather than going back to the previous billing cycle to calculate interest charges. So-called two-cycle or double-cycle billing hurts consumers who pay off their balances, because they are hit with finance charges from the previous cycle even though they have paid the bill in full.

- *Subprime credit cards for people with bad credit*: People who get subprime credit cards and are charged account-opening fees that eat up their available balances get some relief under the new credit-card law. These upfront fees cannot exceed 25 percent of the available credit limit in the first year of the card. Instead of charging high upfront fees, some issuers are considering high interest rates on these high credit-risk accounts.

- *Minimum payments*: Credit-card issuers must disclose to cardholders the consequences of making only minimum payments each month, namely how long it would take to pay off the entire balance if users only made the minimum monthly payment. Issuers must also provide information on how much users must pay each month if they want to pay off their balance in thirty-six months, including the amount of interest.

- *Late-fee restrictions*: Late fees are capped at twenty-five dollars for occasional late payments; however, the fees can be higher if cardholders are late more than once in a six-month period.

- *Gift cards*: Gift cards cannot expire sooner than five years after they are issued. Dormancy fees can only be charged if the card is unused for twelve months or more. Issuers can charge only one fee per month, but there is no limit on the amount of the fee.

Although these reforms represent the most dramatic changes in credit-card laws in decades, they do not protect card users from everything. Issuers can still raise interest rates on future card purchases, and there is no cap on how high interest rates can go. Business and corporate credit cards are not covered by the protections in the CARD Act. If credit-card accounts are based on variable APRs (as the majority now are), interest rates can increase as the prime rate goes up. Credit-card companies can also continue to close accounts and slash credit limits abruptly, without giving cardholders advance warning. Many banks are already finding ways around the law and launching new fees not specifically banned by the credit-card reform law.

Credit Score and Repair

The Reason Codes

When a lender receives your credit score, it includes "score reason codes" to explain the top reasons your score was not higher. These codes can give you an idea of how you should start improving your score, such as closing unused credit accounts or being more diligent about making payments on time.

Lenders are not required to tell you your credit score, but if your score is low and you are turned down for a loan, the lender must give you the reason for your low score. Your score is accompanied by a maximum of four "reason codes" that explain why your score wasn't higher, listed in order of impact on the score. These codes are essential in helping you improve your score. Your four reason codes would be chosen from the following list:

- amount owed on accounts is too high
- delinquency on accounts
- too few bank revolving accounts or recent payment information
- too many bank or national revolving accounts
- too many accounts with balances
- consumer finance accounts
- account payment history is too new to rate
- too many inquiries in last twelve months
- too many accounts opened in last twelve months
- proportion of balances to credit limits is too high
- amount owed on revolving accounts is too high
- length of revolving credit history is too short
- time since delinquency is too recent or unknown
- length of credit history is too short
- lack of recent bank revolving account information
- no recent nonmortgage balance information
- number of accounts with delinquency
- too few accounts currently paid as agreed
- time since derogatory public record or collection
- amount past due on accounts
- serious delinquency, derogatory public record, or collection
- too many bank or national revolving accounts with balances
- no recent revolving balances or bankcard balances
- proportion of loan balances to loan amounts is too high
- lack of recent installment loan information
- date of last inquiry too recent
- time since last account opening too short
- number of revolving accounts
- number of bank revolving or revolving accounts

The Importance of a Good Record-Keeping System

The better your record-keeping system, the better the available information you have to make decisions. Some key documents (this is a partial list only) to keep in a safe place include the following:

- birth certificate
- car titles and registration
- checking- (registers and unused checks) and savings-account statements and information
- credit cards and statements (including debit cards and ATM cards)
- driver's license
- household inventory (item description, cost, when purchased, replacement cost, pictures)
- insurance policies and contact information (life, health, auto, renters, homeowners, long-term disability)
- investment statements—401(k), stocks, mutual funds—and contact information
- legal documents (trusts, power of attorney, wills)
- loans (student, bank) and repayment schedules
- medical records, including prescription information
- mother's birthday (date only) and phone number
- pay stubs and W-2 records
- photo IDs (university, employer, building-access security cards)
- renters contract/lease or mortgage and property deeds
- safe-deposit box (location and key)
- social-security card/records
- tax returns and supporting documents
- warranties and receipts on major purchases

Make a Note:

Make a Note: